DARING HEARTS

DARING HEARTS

Lesbian and Gay Lives
of 50s and 60s Brighton

Brighton Ourstory Project

QueenSpark Book 28

First published in Great Britain by QueenSpark Books,
1992
68 Grand Parade
Brighton
BN2 2JY

British Library cataloguing in Publications Data
A catalogue record of this book is available from the British
Library

ISBN 0 904733 31 9

Printed and bound in Great Britain by
Delta Press, Brighton, East Sussex

For all the voices
that will never be heard

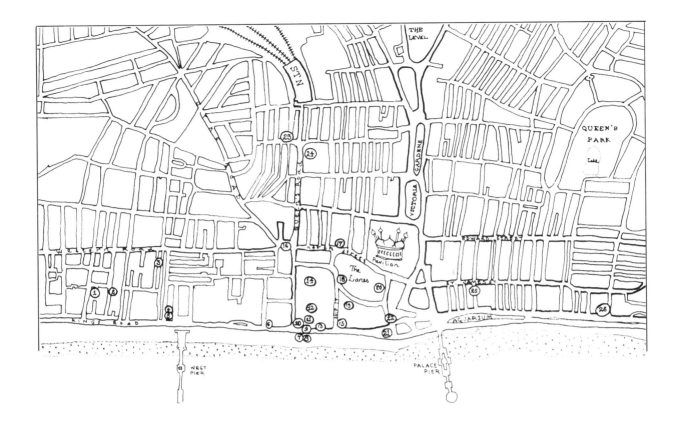

Brighton 1950-1969

1 Minorities Research Group met at 5 Norfolk Buildings.
2 Spartacus Magazine Office, 46 Preston Street.
3 Queen of Clubs, 25 Bedford Square.
4 Regency Club, 5 Regency Square.
5 St Albans Club, 2 Regency Square.
6 Harrison's Bar, 24/25 King's Road.
7 Belvedere, 159/160 King's Rd Arches.
8 Fortune of War, 157 King's Rd Arches.
9 Forty Two Club, 42 King's Road.

10 Chatfield's, 80 West Street.
11 Sherry's Bar, 7 Middle Street.
12 Spotted Dog, 13 Middle Street.
13 Argyle Hotel, 78 Middle Street
14 Variety Club, 35 Middle Street.
15 Heart and Hand, 65 Ship Street.
16 The Quadrant, 12/13 North Street Quadrant.
17 Regina Club, 147 North Street.
18 Lorelei coffee bar, 5 Union Street.
19 Black Lion Street Cottage.

20 Golden Fleece, 1 Market Street.
21 Curtain Club, 3 King's Road.
22 The Greyhound, 74 East Street.
23 Jokers Club, 58 Queen's Road.
24 Unicorn Bookshop, 49 Gloucester Road.
25 Pigott's Bar, 16 Madeira Place.
26 British Legion Club, 76 Marine Parade.

Introduction

I expect you know there is a huge homosexual kingdom just below the
surface of everyday life?[1]   Anonymous gay man. 1960.

This is a book of true-life stories about a special and unique civilisation. It
is drawn from taped interviews with forty lesbians and gay men who speak
openly about their lives in and around Brighton in the fifties and sixties
when that town was enjoying a national reputation as a gay Mecca — as the
place to come.

Brighton offered a degree of freedom which was unusual in Britain at
that time. Word was secretly spreading, passed on small pieces of paper and
whispered from ear to ear. Lesbians and gay men came from all over the
country to holiday and settle down, often seeking refuge from situations of
intolerable homophobia in their home towns. In Brighton, a strong queer
culture was quietly thriving — there were pubs, clubs, cafes, trolling
grounds, parties and, hallelujah, enormous numbers of homosexuals.
Many lesbians and gay men, walking down Queen's Road from the station
felt, for the first time in their lives, like they were coming home.

In the fifties, homosexuality was more widely discussed than ever before.
Lesbians and gay men were bracketed with drug-users, juvenile delinquents,
'immigrants', prostitutes and communists as a 'problem minority' and a
moral threat. Newspapers ran hundreds of column inches of misinformation.
MPs discussed the 'homosexual problem' in Parliament — it was perceived
to be increasing — how should it be treated and stopped? Somehow it was
hoped that homosexuals would disappear, like ghosts in a dark room, in the
strong light of modern medicine and rational political debate.

Male homosexuality was still totally illegal. Gay men were the victims
of vicious police witch-hunts which reached a peak in 1954. Prison sentences
were severe. One of our contributors left the country with his partner at this
time and took up residence in Sweden because a homosexual life in Britain
seemed impossible.

Lesbian sexuality was subject to more subtle controls and social taboos.
Though the law did not at that time specifically mention lesbianism,
nevertheless some legislation could be successfully used to prevent and
control lesbian relationships, as one contributor found when her parents
threatened court action against her lover on a charge of abduction.

Even in Brighton, life was very far from sweet. Very little advice was
available. No gay press. No switchboards. Families, doctors, priests and
straight friends were likely to be hostile or neutrally ignorant. Bosses,
landladies, policemen, even shop assistants could seem at times to be
members of an army, bent on the detection of deviance and its punishment.

Lois Hayden, Soldiers in Skirts, 1951.

Lesbians and gay men were forced to perform miraculous balancing acts between their need for self-expression and the necessity of secrecy. Every homosexual lived with a complex code of discretion — had to decide each day when it was possible to let their hair down, relax, be a little blatant, and when it was necessary to button their lip, lower their voice, guard their glance, act a little straight. In 1948 the following 'Don'ts' were suggested as 'sane and useful advice for male inverts':

> Don't commit to writing any admissions as to your inclinations; don't masquerade - on any occasion whatsover - in women's clothes, take female parts in theatrical performances, or use make-up; don't be too meticulous in the matter of your own clothes, or affect extremes in colour or cut; don't wear conspicuous rings, watches, cuff-links, or other jewellery; don't allow your voice or intonation to display feminine inflection - cultivate a masculine tone and method of expression; don't stand with your hand on your hip, or walk mincingly; don't become identified with the groups of inverts which form in every city; don't let it be noticed that you are bored by female society; don't persuade yourself into thinking that love is the same as friendship; don't become involved with men who are not of your age or set; don't let your enthusiasm for particular male friends make you conspicuous in their eyes, or in the eyes of society; don't occupy yourself with work or pastimes which are distinctly feminine; don't, under any circumstances, compromise yourself by word or action with strangers.[2]

After the advances of the last twenty years, it's almost impossible to understand what life was really like under these conditions. What did it feel like to be engaged in ceaseless lies and wangles? Listening with one ear for a footstep on the stair. Watching ourselves for the tell-tale signs of our desires and locking them away. At times the stories in this book sound like tales of life in an occupied country, of the Resistance movement in German-occupied France.

The psychological effects of living as a sexual criminal, under such pressure, are impossible to measure. Some were strong enough. For others it was a 'bloody and helpless life'.[3] Problems of low self-esteem, loneliness and depression seem to have been common.

However, the later fifties and sixties saw a gradual process of social liberation. Some taboos were broken and a few rules relaxed. The laws on abortion, capital punishment, censorship, divorce, licensing and gambling were liberalised. Many gay men joined the Homosexual Law Reform Society which had been formed in 1958 to campaign discreetly and cautiously for the implementation of the Wolfenden Report's recommendation that male homosexuality be partially decriminalised. Eventually in 1967 the Sexual Offences Act legalised consenting sexual behaviour, in private, between two men of twenty-one years and over. In itself this was a limited freedom and very few of our male contributors remember the '67 Act as an important moment in their lives.

In 1963, the Minorities Research Group — Britain's first public organisation for lesbians — was formed. The MRG held regular meetings in London and produced a magazine — Arena Three — which, as this country's first openly gay magazine, produced by and for gay people, can be regarded as the mother of all the magazines, male or female, which have followed. The South Coast group was based in Brighton at 5 Norfolk Buildings, Sillwood Street and organised valuable counselling, advice and social events for lesbians who would otherwise have had nowhere to turn.

A revival of the organised feminist movement was stirring in the United States. Betty Friedan and Simone de Beauvoir were widely read. But even in the fifties many lesbians had been seeking to lead fulfilled and autonomous lives. They were actively fighting to pursue their own careers, run their own homes and move independently in a man's world.

A growing number of books on gay themes were being passed from hand to hand and read until they fell apart. Some were sensational pulp novels, others such as Maureen Duffy's The Microcosm or Rodney Garland's The Heart in Exile were sensitive treatments of gay life by lesbian and gay authors. On television, dramas and documentaries were attempting serious coverage of the subject and Nancy Spain was strutting her fearlessly butch stuff. On the Home Service, Jules and Sandy were treating the unsuspecting listeners of Round the Horne to bravura displays of polari. On the stage, the huge glam drag shows which followed the original 'Soldiers in Skirts' gave queans an unparalleled opportunity to camp themselves gutless in front of a paying audience. Plays like Five Finger Exercise (1958) by Peter Shaffer and The Boys in the Band (1969) by Mart Crowley broke new ground. In the cinema, Victim (1961), The Loudest Whisper (1962) and The Killing of Sister George (1969) drew huge lesbian and gay audiences. In 1967, the first of the gay male magazines appeared — TIMM followed by Spartacus and Jeremy — replacing the discreet nudge-nudge, wink-wink muscle magazines of the fifties.

Britain was moving from post-war austerity towards an idea of a 'permissive society'. Books, films, meetings, legislation, small acts of public courage together made a huge impression on lesbian and gay life. A movement towards radical change was growing. The seeds were sown for the flowering of the liberation movement of the early seventies. A new openness. Life would not be the same again. In 1950, it would have been unthinkable to speak of a mass homosexual love demonstration, as an anonymous lesbian was reported as suggesting in 1964:

> I think the thing to do would be for all these millions of homosexuals, rising up to put an end to the oppression once and for all, to make love in the streets. That would be the final and logical challenge wouldn't it? And society couldn't do a damned thing if ten to fifteen million people were involved. We might sweep away the rest of the old sex prejudices along with the persecution of our own people. I think, I sincerely think, that if something like that happened, then history would regard it as one of the most brave and wonderful things that any group of human beings has ever done.[4]

In Brighton, the official bodies hold no records of lesbian and gay life from 1950 to 1969. It's a dislocating experience to visit Brighton Borough Council, Brighton Reference Library, Brighton Museum and find nothing. It's as though lesbians and gay men have not existed, have made no contribution to the culture and economy of the town. Are we all ghosts then, muttering in dark corners and whispering in the wind? In Section 28 Britain, institutions cannot be trusted to tell the story of our lives.

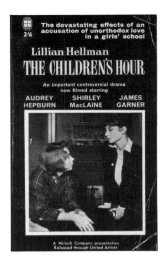

Lillian Hellman's 'The Children's Hour', filmed as 'The Loudest Whisper'.

Emergency oral history work is urgently needed. Every lesbian and every gay man is a walking library of information on our life and times. This information does not exist outside our heads. Our passions and experiences are worth preserving for future generations. They will want to know about our lives.

But contacting forty people who were prepared to record their experiences for this book was a difficult and sometimes harrowing experience. Many lesbians and gay men are, in some way, scarred by the events of their lives in the fifties and sixties. They are rightly mistrustful of unsympathetic exposure. It has been a matter of slowly establishing trust and relying on word of mouth contact. There are many people we would like to have included but were unable to reach. Of those we did reach, one lesbian contributor pulled out at a late stage, assisted by a member of a lay catholic organisation.

We have seldom failed to be moved by the stories we were told. These forty lesbians and gay men have responded with remarkable bravery, wisdom, humour and grace to the difficulties they have faced. Lesbian and gay life now is deeply shaped by the courage and sacrifices of the queers who lived through that time. We would like this book to serve as a reminder of their hard-won experience and as evidence of their continued survival. We hope the stories collected here together form a vivid panorama of a remarkable community of people at a remarkable time in Brighton's — and Britain's — history.

In those days, freedom was not something we were given. It was something we had to steal. In the eyes of the law, we were all sex criminals, handlers of stolen goods. 'Daring Hearts' aims to celebrate our hidden pleasures and commemorate our 'crime'.

Brighton Ourstory Project
March 1992.

1. A Minority: A Report on the Life of the Male Homosexual in Great Britain. Gordon Westwood. Longmans. London. 1960
2. The Invert and his Social Adjustment. Anomaly. Bailliere, Tindall and Cox. London. 1948.
3. Chorus of Witches. Paul Buckland. W. H. Allen. London. 1959.
4. The Homosexual Revolution. R. E. L. Masters. Belmont Books. New York City. 1964.

Of course, those were the days of the trolleybuses. Clean streets. Mods and rockers. Milk bars. Man-made fabrics. Cheap drinks. White lip-stick. White weddings. Pointy bras. Sex scandals. Paddle steamers. Illegal abortions. Capital punishment. Johnnie Ray. Dusty Springfield. The West Pier. Policemen in white summer helmets. Basement discotheques. Kinky boots. Weirdy hair-dos. Dave Clarke Five shirts. Austin Metropolitans. The Pill. Pink Cadillacs. Purple Hearts. Short hair and sideboards. The sound of seagulls. I remember the taste of salt on my lover's skin, lying in our bedsit room, after one hot day on the beach, summer 1955. Life was sweet.

And in the Aquarium Palais Ballroom, midnight approaches - Ladies and Gentlemen! The Cascade of Two Thousand Balloons! Take your partners for the last dance.

Gone are those days.

SANDIE: We came down on holiday, a week's holiday and it was the *freedom* in Brighton. There were so many gay people and they seemed to be accepted and there were clubs for gay people . . . ohh, wonderful! It was absolutely Mecca because it was very gay then. Brighton's gay now but it was very, very gay then.

We'd never seen gay people *en masse* like that before and clubs that everyone knew were clubs for gay people which was unknown, even in a great city like Birmingham, but there you are. We actually saw gay boys that we could identify as gay boys walking in couples along the shopping streets and that's fascinating. And of course there was the sea and the sand, well, not sand at Brighton, but the Downs and all of this and it just seemed like everything, everything was there and we loved it. And we made up our minds straight away that we would move down.

PAT: When I came to Brighton I discovered that there were real bars only for men who liked other men. And that there were a lot of these kind of men here. And so I suddenly found myself like a pig in clover. I was here in paradise, a paradise which in my wildest dreams I'd never seen as possible. Everything went on secretly but at the same time it was there. And it was a wonderful world, this secret world behind closed doors, like Alice going through the Looking Glass into Wonderland. If you didn't know where to get in you didn't get in, and I was perhaps twenty-three, twenty-four before I found the way into it, which basically was here in Brighton.

GILL: Auntie's was a very well-known gay pub in Walsall. I was the only woman there. That was in 1956. They said if I came down to Brighton the streets were lined with girls. I could just have my choice, go anywhere I wanted, they were all over the place. And I thought, 'Well, let's go down there.'

SIOBHAN: There were things about the Gateways that irritated me so I liked to go to different places and Brighton was on the main line train and it had the sea and the Downs, which attracted me, and I could leave my grotty bedsits, I could leave my grotty jobs behind, I could leave any pettiness and in-fighting I had with whoever in the Gateways or whatever club was in in London and I could còme down here and get away from my peer group for a start. Brighton was just very welcoming and I wasn't aware of being Irish, I just was, I was allowed to be. I had no sense of threat in Brighton as opposed to London in those days. And so Brighton represented for me an escapism from my own anger, from the struggle of my own life.

> 66 **Everybody would go there. Queans from all over England would come down to Brighton for a camp weekend. Brighton was probably the most outrageous place in the country.** JAMES 99

13

I had a different feel about myself when I was down here . . . I preferred myself . . . there wasn't that sense of stress that there seemed to be with London at all.

KAY: When I moved to Brighton from Hampstead in 1968, I came to live in Arundel Terrace. Talk about gay Brighton! It was like being back in Hampstead, in a way, except it was gayer. There was definitely a greater mix in Hampstead but here it was cliquey. If you went to one of the parties it would be mostly gay people.

TED: I found it very difficult in Southampton because I didn't really have anybody close to talk to about it, I had to cope with it on my own and it wasn't happy at times. I can remember when I was fifteen, sixteen going to bed crying and thinking I was ill and different to other people, in short, I felt very much an outcast. But when I came to Brighton . . . not knowing at that point that Brighton was the gay capital of the South Coast. Looking back on it, I suppose I felt a bit euphoric, I didn't have to conform, I could just be myself and there was no restrictions and I just dived in and never looked back.

AILEEN: When I came down here, into Hove, I could not believe the freedom women had. Because what I had seen was totally different back home in Glasgow. There were restrictions, you were responsible, you were a provider. Down here it was like a new life, you know, it was something that was totally new to me, and I loved it. You could go out on a Sunday in a pair of slacks, really enjoy it. Nobody turned around calling you a cow.

GEORGE: It's an odd thing because I've always known I was gay, there's never been any question of that. When I was a kid I always liked dolls. I mean I wanted a doll. There was a shop at the top of George Street which sold limbs, you know, you could buy bits of dolls. And I would save my sixpences, buy an arm one week, a leg next week. And I loved black dolls, don't know why, but I wanted a black doll. And I had several of these things and they were dressed, and they were looked after, and they had acorns for water bottles, the works. And if a girl had a doll I liked, I would steal it if I could; I was quite avaricious about dolls. Well, my father bought me, funnily enough, what I call a fairy cycle with two wheels. Well, two wheels was too masculine for me, I still wanted my three-wheeler. I got on this bike and my father was really funny with me about teaching me and he was a butch man, my old man — he'd die if he was alive today — I went off on this bike, went off down the road, and I saw this girl with this wondrous doll's pram. It was everything I ever wanted you know, it was the Rolls-Royce of doll's prams as far as I was concerned. So we did a swap. So I went back with my doll's pram. I was delighted. My father was apoplectic. I can still remember. 'What sort of fucking kid have we got here?' he said. 'Goes out with a bloody bicycle and comes back here with a fucking pram.' My mother's going, 'Well, he'll get out of it one day.' Well, that went on all my life.

VICKY: I was attracted to girls, but I didn't know why. And at that time I was mixing with a whole crowd of girls, some considerably older than myself. And one of the places we went, one of the girls, her father was an undertaker and they had this enormous premises with all these coffins in it and I decided that we were gonna have a secret society. We all had to wear cloaks and masks and everything else and we all had these strange names, but we played in this area where they built these coffins and we used to frighten ourselves to death. We'd hide and we'd go down there and it would be quite dark in this place and you'd suddenly hear this creaking and the bloody coffin lid'd come up. Oh God, we nearly killed ourselves with this. Anyway, one of the older girls that used to come down used to always call me 'Butch'. I used to say, 'Why do you call me Butch?' They said, 'Oh well, you'll understand, when you get older. . .'

PATRICK: When I was about twelve or thirteen I remember watching a Peter Sellers film, in Brighton, I think it was 'The Wrong Arm of the Law'. It was an old Ealing film, and he played a double part as a con-man, and also as a very camp couturier, in a dress shop in Regent Street. But it was really over-the-top, and that was the first time I'd ever seen camp. I didn't even know what the word meant. And he had all these gorgeous clothes and the effeminate mannerisms. And I remember walking down the street one day in front of my mother and my brother, sort of mincing down the street. And my mother said, 'Do you have to walk down the street like that?' And I said, 'No, I'm perfectly alright.' I was a little Quentin Crisp at thirteen. And she said, 'Have you ever heard of the word "queer"?' And I said, 'Yes.' And so I carried on and she didn't say anything. When I'd seen that film, it was like I wanted to be a part of that. I thought, 'I belong to all that world.' Well, I hope no-one would describe me as a screaming old quean but it was like a drug, you wanted to be a part of it.

SIOBHAN: Certainly by my teens I thought, 'I must be what they call a lesbian.' I decided, 'I'm *that*. It's it. I'm going to be tall and have crinkly hair.' That's what I'd read lesbians looked like in the Observer supplement or something. All the Sunday newspapers used to be in the house and I read a supplement. It was a really nice article about two women living together and that was the first time I came across the word lesbian and I took the article out of the paper. I used to wear jeans in those days and I had it in my back pocket. It was my secret. And then one day my mother said, 'Where's that piece gone from the newspaper? I wanted to read it.' And I'm going, 'I don't know where it is, I don't know.' And it was crinkledy and it was all falling apart. I had it for a long time in my back pocket. It was something special and I held it close, I had an identity; something became clear to me from that article.

PATRICK: I can remember when I came home one day when I was about thirteen, and I brought a copy of 'The Naked Lunch' by William

Sunday Times colour supplement, 1965.

15

Burroughs, and a copy of 'Justine' by the Marquis de Sade, and my father, being utterly heterosexual, wasn't in the slightest bit bothered about the Marquis de Sade. He thought that it was quite wholesome reading and he wanted to read it himself. But he was a bit perturbed that I was reading 'The Naked Lunch' because he thought it was a poof's book.

JAMES: I lodged with relatives here in Brighton for several years which was interesting. I never knew how much they knew, they never said a word, never. There was a schoolboy that used to share the holidays with me. In those days working-class families didn't have such things as single beds so there was a double bed job and as we grew older so we grew bolder and all sorts of explorations and games went on. It was only years later I realised that the wall between our bedroom and theirs was thin match boarding and so, with whispers and things, I think they must have been aware of things going on. But to them, so what? What was forbidden in those days was for boys and girls to do things together and the girl to get pregnant because she would be in disgrace. Even in the fifties it was a considerable disgrace. Therefore I think a lot of working-class people, providing they didn't know what was going on, they didn't mind if you put two boys in a bed together and two girls in a bed together. Then no-one could get pregnant.

❤   ❤   ❤

BOBBY: I identified very strongly with male pin-ups, I mean when I was at school I used to draw handsome men all the time because that was supposed to be me, you see. I was identifying with masculinity I think. I used to draw pictures of these handsome men. Other girls were drawing ballerinas and horses and I was drawing these handsome men. The fantasies were that I was the handsome man, of course, and I was able to sweep women off their feet and carry them off into the night.

JANICE: Most people tended to go for the games teacher. I thought she was perfectly hideous, all sinew and whiskers, you know. I don't think they've changed much, have they? All sinew and whiskers, yuk. There were two teachers there who were living together. Now the older of the two, looking at her from a thirteen year old's eyes, was a very aggressive, unpleasant, snappy, vinegary old prat. The younger of the two taught history. Well, I came top in history throughout my school years. I actually passed my GCE, my A level, I took a degree in history and I'm sure it was all down to being madly in love with Miss Marchant, who is probably dead now, but Miss Marchant, who was the history teacher, wonderful woman, lovely, lovely face. Yes, I remember it vividly.

SIOBHAN: I went to an all girls convent and there was a group in my class that suddenly started getting into boyfriends. I continued in my hockey and games bit but I felt pressurised by this group. And it was, who do I like, who do I like? So I picked this really sickly bloke that I liked. First I picked the one that everyone liked so that I'd have no chance of getting near him, then I picked this horrible one that was really wimpish. And I used to walk down the road with him when everyone paired off and walked down the road with their boyfriends.

PATRICK: When I was at school the Spotted Dog was the only place that was known as a queer bar; wasn't known as a gay bar 'cause we didn't use the word gay then. But it was a dare at school for 2/6d if you dared to go through the door, not to buy a drink, but if you actually dared to go through the door. But if anyone wanted to take the piss out of you at school they'd say, 'Oh you know Patrick Newley's been to the Spotted Dog.' None of us ever, I don't think, ever had the nerve. It was even a sort of nerve to go into the same street as the Spotted Dog. But that was the only place that we knew that was gay. It was sort of frightening.

The Spotted Dog.

JAMES: The randy boys who had always got their hand up other boys' trousers are the ones that ten years later were married and pushing prams. They were sexy rather than gay, just highly sexed, but there were all sorts of things going on. It was just considered that it was the natural occupation of boys to be playing either with themselves or with the others. I can remember one very randy boy with a very big dick whose name I can't recall, just as well, he would actually sit at the back of the class wanking and when he came he would lift the desk lid and shoot into the desk! I mean, he was quite outrageous, this enormous thing. And I can remember a maths master, Joe Rees, looking up one day very wearily and saying, 'Put it away, Macaulay, put it away.' It does seem since, that the boys who have grown to be gay were probably the ones who were too nervous to do much when they were kids.

JANICE: I was totally repressed at that age, thirteen, fourteen. I just went along with the mob and said how interested I was in Cliff Richard, when as far as I was concerned he could have walked off the pier and I wouldn't have missed him. Dusty Springfield, well the Springfields as it was then — mm! I liked Connie Francis too, and Patsy Cline. I had pin-ups, all women, would you believe? Then one day, shows what you think like when you're that age, but it suddenly occurred to me that I'd only got women on the wall. So I had to very quickly find an Elvis Presley or two and a James Dean and a Cliff Richard and bung them up with them, just for good measure. That's absolutely true.

SHEILA: When I left school, I started as an apprentice hairdresser and I got very friendly with my employer's daughter, who was about the same age as me. We became very fond of one another. I hadn't got a clue that if you kissed another girl it was wrong. I mean, I liked her, she liked me, we shared things. We went everywhere together and I think we kissed each other good-bye. Her mother decided that was it — she wasn't going to have me working there any longer so I was given my notice. I didn't understand why, because I thought what I was doing was perfectly natural.

JANINE: When I was sixteen and a half I wanted very much to get away from home, and somebody had come to St Mary's Hall, a recruiting

"I know I used to wander round at night when I was fourteen, used to go out for walks every night wondering if I'd ever get picked up. But I didn't really know about gay bars. I wouldn't have had the nerve to have knocked on the door of the Spotted Dog. But I always dreamt that someone would sweep me off my feet.
PATRICK **"**

sergeant for the Women's Royal Army Corps and I was very attracted, without knowing why, to the idea of this amazing thing where I could drive. I was very envious of my mother's motor racing career and spent my childhood surrounded by huge silver cups that she had won. And I wanted to be a driver too, but at sixteen and a half I was too young. So I got something called an ink eradicater and forged my birth certificate, altered it so that I was born in 1933 instead of 1934, which made me in fact seventeen and a half, and I went up to the recruiting office outside Brighton station and signed on and went home and said, 'Whoopee, I know I'm only sixteen and a half, I know I'm at public school but I'm off to the WRAC!'

PATRICK: I remember, I was actually asked to leave school, when I was in the fifth year. I wasn't expelled but they said it was about time I went, you know. Well, I remember walking out of the school and thinking, 'Will I ever have sex again?' 'Cause I was sort of thrown out into the world of Brighton and, of course, I'd never heard of gay bars or anything like that. The first time I had what I would call *real* sex — 'cause everything else before that had been sort of wanking about under the desks and in cupboards in school — but the first time I ever had real sex, I was seduced when I was fifteen and it was a friend of my father's, who came to stay at the house. He would have been about thirty-five or something.

My mother and father had gone to bed and this bloke was watching television with me and I can always remember what the name of the programme was, it was 'All Night Wrestling' with Mick McManus and he said, 'Have you ever been fucked?' And I said, 'Oh yes! Many, many times.' Well, you have to say that sort of thing. So he went up the stairs and he went to get some Vaseline and he came down again and he said, 'You know what this is?' I said, 'Oh yes. I know all about this.' I'd never been fucked by anyone in my life, you know. And so he screwed me with the Vaseline, dear, while Mick McManus was on the telly and my parents were upstairs and my brother was asleep upstairs. And I enjoyed every moment of it until it was over and then I had the most shocking guilt of all time. And he said, 'Well, don't you want to stick around and have a coffee?' I ran away to my bedroom and I felt that I was going to die and that I'd committed sin and all my Roman Catholic background came back to me and I was almost praying to God.

Well, I was commuting from Brighton to London and I was working in Better Books in Charing Cross Road. Fortunately there was this wonderful old quean that used to be the manager of the shop and I poured my heart out to him next day and he was wonderful because he turned round to me and he said, 'Oh well, you don't want to worry about that, dear. I mean, it's your first time, there'll be plenty of others, dear.' And I went back on the train in the evening and I thought to myself, 'Well, I dunno, I sort of quite enjoyed it really.' So all the guilt was lifted completely by that old quean who was about seventy or something like that. So, if it wasn't for that old quean, I'd have gone through life with a terrible guilt.

SIOBHAN: I'd written to Marjorie Proops and it took three months for an answer. She wrote back saying, 'Don't worry, dear, you'll grow out of it' and I sat there and sobbed. I sobbed my heart out over that woman. There were two things that I'd written about. I think I'd said something like, 'I think I'm lesbian and also I don't like men near me, I don't like boys and I don't want physical contact with men . . .' and she'd dismissed me in this one line . . . and I just felt like screaming, it was awful.

JANINE: She was about thirty at the time that I was sixteen and leaving home and she was bisexual but she never made any move towards me. But she used to say things like, 'Janine, I'm very partial to you.' And that sort of gave me frissons of delight. I don't think she ever married. She was having this affair, she was potty about this man, Carroll Gibbons, this band leader, who played at the Savoy but she had certainly had lots of girlfriends, and she sussed me out. I mean, she knew more about me than I possibly knew about myself.

She was extremely wealthy, lived in Sussex Square, absolutely next door. My mother disapproved of her greatly and she was a rather, sort of, wonderfully decadent writer and she had built for herself, in this house, a wonderful studio downstairs because she was mad about all music but particularly somebody called Nellie Lutcher. And she used to take me down and say, 'I will teach you to dance.' She taught me to dance and we used to dance together night after night to Nellie Lutcher, 'That Fine Brown Frame'. I can hear it now. She was a very well-read, clever woman who knew, obviously, that I was gay and was going to be gay and knew that I was a lesbian.

We were on Black Rock, one of the beaches at Black Rock, one day after I'd decided to go into the WRAC, on the pebbles, and she said, 'Janine, there is something that I must tell you, if you're going to join the WRAC. There are these women, called lesbians.' And I honestly thought that she said 'thespians' and I spent three very, very confused years after that conversation because I really thought the word 'thespian' meant lesbian. And I had really no idea. I thought this was marvellous, that there were other women like me because I'd always been totally gay. It was very easy to be gay. It wasn't a hassle or a problem, certainly not at the age of sixteen and a half going into the WRAC, where practically everybody was gay. I mean, all the women were gay.

BOBBY: I didn't want to put a name to it at all because, in Catholic surroundings, you're not supposed to deviate in that way. So I really felt a lot of guilty conflict, for a long time. The sensational pressure that one had, to do something about it. I needed help. I just had to say something. I had to talk about it. She was the secretary of the local art college I first went to. She worked as a secretary there. But she lived with her parents just over the road from where we lived and she used to come and visit sometimes for a cup of tea. She was somebody I trusted, I mean, we all did. For all the young art students at their first art college, the secretary plays a kind of mother role. And I think that's what it was. I certainly couldn't have talked to my mother about it at that stage. I think that I told her because she'd also been in the forces and I'd heard that people who had been in the women's

> ❝ I got into a terrible state. I didn't know whether I was supposed to be a man or a woman or what I was supposed to be. I didn't know how to behave. And I had nobody to turn to, to help me. VALERIE ❞

army have come across this thing, they know about it.

I think I just said to her, very tentatively, that I felt that I was attracted towards females, other females, because we did life drawing at the art college. I was drawing the human form, especially the female form. It was drawn with tenderness and sensitivity and passion. I wasn't looking at the human form, I was feeling it. And some of them were very sensual drawings, without being overtly sexual. The reason that my life drawing was quite good at that time was because of all this repressed desire, I think. I've always thought in terms of drawing as being some sort of capture. It's a sort of desire, seeing something that you want to hold, you know. So that's what I told her and she was duly shocked!

First of all she warned me against it. She said, 'Good heavens, you're going to meet some very strange people in this sort of world.' But she introduced me to another person that she knew and that led me into an easy kind of relationship that broke down the terrible block.

SIOBHAN: When I was twenty-one, I had an Irish friend who worked in an office and she came back and said, 'Guess what, we've got a lesbian working in our office.' I just wanted to know everything that this lesbian did, everything. Every day that I saw this Irish friend, we just talked about Rita all the time. And then I asked her if she'd arrange for me to meet Rita and so this was arranged. We were going to meet in a cafe and I turned up on time, absolutely scared stiff and Rita identified herself and I thought, 'God, she's so attractive.' She would have been about thirty but to me she looked really mature. And she had a grey trouser suit on, which was fashionable in those days and she just looked gorgeous. I asked her if she would take me down to her club, 'cause I knew she went to a club. And she said, 'No,' she didn't think so 'cause she really wanted to persuade me not to be a lesbian, as it's a very lonely and hard life. If she could talk me out of it, she'd rather do that. And I said, 'I don't want talking out, I want to go to the club. Would you take me to the club?' So she said, 'Yes.'

JOHN: I was about eighteen when I first heard the word 'homosexual' when I talked to a close friend who wasn't himself gay. At that time I was very much involved in the evangelical branch of the Christian Church and so was he. I told him that I was very worried about not liking girls like other guys do, and in fact finding men attractive. And he said, 'You're what's called a homosexual' and I said, 'A what?' He said, 'A homosexual. That's the word you use to describe men who like other men.' He said, 'But there's not many of them about, you're perhaps unique.' And so I went on my way, thinking, 'Well, I'm unique and it would be nice to find another guy who's also unique.' I went all through college and I had always the most marvellous love affairs with other guys but we never had sex because we just didn't know that that was possible. I mean, it just didn't seem to be part of it.

SANDIE: We went to see these fireworks and it was a display, so the public were kept back from it, for safety. We were all pressed quite close

Vera's girlfriend, Margaret.

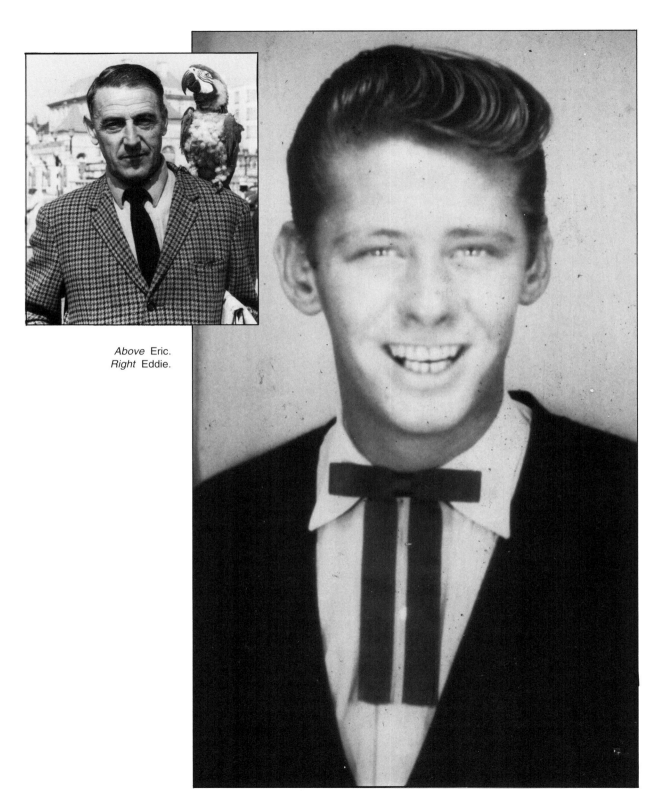

Above Eric.
Right Eddie.

together. She was taller than me and she'd pushed me in front of her, so that I could see quite clearly. I was in the middle of watching this, without any thought in my head, and suddenly I became intensely aware of her standing slightly behind me, at my shoulder. It was like some sort of electric current going backwards and forwards. And my knees went to jelly, oh, a most peculiar sensation. And yet she'd said nothing and done nothing. It just happened. And as we walked away — and I wasn't a bold character at that age, I mean, I was only seventeen — we walked away when it had finished, I took her hand. And that was the beginning of everything. And I've never looked back from that, I was never interested in boys after that.

MICHAEL: I remember the first gay party I ever went to, it was all men, quite a lot of people there, and they were dancing. I couldn't get this together at all because at that time, of course, you used to dance like ballroom type dancing, holding each other, which I found really quite odd. I found it freaky, in fact. I really felt that I had sunk to the lowest depths of, you know, shockness. I got very drunk and finished up in bed with the two blokes who were running the party.

VICKY: He said, 'Would you like to come to a club?' So I said, 'Yeah.' I didn't know what 'a club' was. So he took us to this place and we went in and after about five minutes, I thought, 'These aren't men, they're women dressed in men's clothes!' and I said to Jean, 'Here, these are all women, they're not men!' Well, I couldn't believe my eyes. It suddenly began to gel that there were other women in this world that actually danced with women and they were kissing, and I couldn't believe this. I thought, 'This is wonderful!'

AILEEN: My sister and her husband took me to a club, just down from Brighton station, I think it was called the Jokers Club. And they took me there one night, and there was what I thought was a chap, up at the bar, and I thought, 'God he's handsome.' And it wasn't a chap, it was a girl! I couldn't *believe* it! I thought my sister was having me on. She knew the person and they came over and spoke and when the person spoke it was quite a feminine voice. I couldn't believe there was such a thing. And I thought that I was going to look like that. When people started realising that I was gay, and saw that I was gay, I thought there must be all neon signs all round me! My God! Everybody knows I'm gay! And I didn't know how to react to it.

JOHN: I remember going home to my family, having come to the decision in the early years of living in Brighton that I should not any longer make a secret of being different from other guys — this was before law reform, long before — and I told my mother. 'Now I've told you the truth about myself,' I said, 'now I want you to tell me, will it make any difference to our relationship?' And I remember till now her exact words. She said, 'John, I'm still your mother, you're still my son.' She said, 'I've always been your

> **"** One bloke's much the same as another if you don't want them in the first place. JANICE **"**

mother and I always will be and I still love you as much as I ever did. Which is an awful lot.' And she said, 'The only difference that it will make is that now I respect you more than I ever did before, because you've told me the truth about something that I have always known.'

JOCELYN: I told my mother eventually because I found myself telling her a lot of lies about what I was doing in my life and I wasn't in the habit of lying to her. I thought, 'Why should I do this? I'll tell her.' As I knew she had some gay friends, I thought she would understand, but she just didn't, she just cut off. I don't think it helped that at that time I was with a girl she couldn't stand and she couldn't stand her. I think if I had been with somebody she liked it might have been a bit easier. But I think she probably put together in her mind that I had been led astray or influenced by her, which wasn't true at all, of course, but she didn't know about my previous affairs. So she probably blamed it all on my friend and because she didn't like her the whole thing was, to her, quite wrong.

GRANT: Amongst the general population it was talked about with bated breath, behind raised hands and a normal middle-class family would be *horrified* to think or to know that their son was found to be a homosexual. The mother would object very strongly because she wouldn't become a grandmother and the father would object very strongly because he couldn't kick the ball about with his son on the football pitch. Equally they would be devastated to know that their lovely, beautiful daughter was a lesbian because she wouldn't be producing, she wouldn't be carrying the name on. It wasn't a thing that the public really knew much about. Homosexuality was almost considered an illness. If you took certain pills you could get better from it. 'Oh, he or she must be treated, send them to the doctor.'

JANICE: My best friend at school who would dearly have loved to be on the gay scene and should have been really but, because of parental pressure and fear, I think, fear of being found out, married a local boy and has grown fat and miserable ever since.

SANDIE: I had boyfriends and I was even engaged when I changed over to being gay and the reason was continual parental interference. My mother's greatest fear was that I was going to become pregnant and bring disgrace on the family, because it was a sort of shock/horror thing in those days, getting pregnant, and mother couldn't think of anything more awful than her daughter coming home pregnant. And so there was constant interference in my life.

GEORGE: Well, there was once, when we lived in Braemore Road, my mother was slagging Steve off one Sunday morning to me when he wasn't there. And I went out and I said, 'Get this and get this straight now. Steve is the most important thing in my life. He's more important than you, more important than anything in this world, and you must never, never, say things like that about him to me.' I said, 'Because if it's a question of who goes, it's you.' And that was the end of it. We never discussed it again.

VALERIE: My mother said to the neighbours, 'Course, I have to have a poodle 'cause I'm never going to get any grandchildren. I've got to have something.' I just stood there with a silly smile on my face. Thought 'Tough!'

JO: My mum came to terms with it, she used to say, 'Don't mind you wearing men's clothes, if only you'd wear high-heeled shoes so they could see you were a woman.' That sort of thing. The neighbours used to say, 'How is it your Josie's not getting married? Isn't it time? What is she, some sort of freak?' By that time I'd had my hair cut off, and that. 'Is she alright? Is she, is she natural down there?' And my mum was ever so good, she'd say, 'Course she is, but she's a career woman, she's not interested in marriage and children, she's not gonna be like her old mum, dependent on men all her life.' Now this was from a very, very normal, fluffy, twice-married, helpless woman. She couldn't do anything, she wasn't even terribly good at the housewife bit. So, I mean, considering nobody taught her what to say and she didn't know anything about anything, she was very, very good.

VERA: I kept going back to my sister; she was normal. I had about four different girlfriends and each time it was going to be the last one — but they were really normal, most of them. They were going round the queer clubs and obviously they used to go with you as an affair and you thought, 'Ohh, lovely, this is it.' Oh, the times I got broken-hearted. Each time I went back to my sister and cried my eyes out, she didn't come out with me but she'd say, 'Never mind, we'll make the bedroom for you here, we'll make a bedroom for you and you can stay.' I just used to act normally, like. But my sister didn't say, 'Because you're unnatural, because you're queer.' She used to say, 'Oh, she'll come back.' But it never came out of her mouth, I don't think she could say to me, 'You're gay.'

GERALD: I always thought that if my parents wanted me to live at home, I must have a little licence. Otherwise, this is why people leave home, because they feel that they are imprisoned, and restricted, and they can't have people staying. I made that decision quite early, and I never asked permission, I used to say, 'Oh, well, I've got Fred,' or whoever it was, 'and they'll be staying on Thursday.' And there was never any question. Had there been problems about it, I should certainly have rented a flat. And my parents would have lost — I hope it was a pleasure that I remained at home, they certainly gave me to understand that it was — they would have lost my company, and only had visits from me, which is not what they wanted. So it was never discussed, never discussed. They probably discussed it between themselves but it was never discussed openly, and I think my mother preferred it that way. She didn't wish to have it underlined and confirmed. I think that was the attitude with most parents, in those days.

VERA: I never told my family, it never came out in my family. But I felt they knew, I didn't try to pretend. Had my father come out and said, 'Why don't you want a boyfriend . . . ?' At that time I daren't because I used to get hidings anyway and if I'd said to him, 'Because I don't like boys,' he'd have probably slaughtered me.

> **Some kind person told my father that I was queer and he said I wasn't to have anything to do with my young brother. I don't know what he thought I was going to do to my brother, I'm sure.** SHEILA

BUCK: It was a closed shop as far as my father was concerned and he went on as if it never existed. We never discussed it until a few weeks before he died and I said then, 'There was something I've always wanted to say.' And he said, 'I know what it is. I knew all along.' So I said, 'You never discussed it with me. I've lived in a blank world. We could have had so much fun talking or having someone to understand.' I said, 'The only person was my mother and I don't think she really understood, she just, sort of, was a good listener.' And he said, 'I . . . all I can say is, I'm sorry.'

SANDIE: My parents turned up in Brighton out of the blue. Oh, my God, that was terrifying! They rang me from Brighton seafront, from somewhere near the Aquarium, and I was so lucky because they couldn't find me. They couldn't find Grand Parade, they couldn't find where I was living with my girlfriend, so they rang to say, 'WE'RE HERE, DARLING! But we can't find you.' Thank God for that! Oh! Because, I mean, they thought I'd moved down on my own, you see, and so, the next fifteen minutes, the world went mad. We were *tearing* up and down stairs removing all my girlfriend's clothes from the room because we were afraid that they might come back. Do you know, they never did. I went down to the seafront to meet them so it was all, all for nothing.

JANINE: When I was in the WRAC I went in as a raw recruit and then I wanted to drive, so I became a driver, which meant driving ten ton lorries around the Wrekin in Shropshire and doing exciting things like that. My first serious girlfriend was a woman called Al and when I went home on leave she used to write to me in Brighton. Knowing my mother was extremely inquisitive, I invented this boyfriend called Al because Al is such a masculine name, it's terribly easy. And my mother, this is a shameful story and she was a shameful woman, read the letters when I was out one day and realised from something in the letters that this was a woman writing to me and not a man. And my mother went absolutely hysterical and the doctor was called. She went to bed for a week. She said she had read these letters, 'I have torn them up and put them down the lavatory, Janine.' And I thought, 'How dare she read my letters!' I was very, very angry about that but I was frightened at the affect it had on my mother. I was still only seventeen, eighteen.

The Aquarium entrance pavilion.

SHEILA: I had to do what I was told to do by my parents; whether I wanted to or not, I just had to do it. I think I withdrew into myself, that was my way out of it. I think I was looking for someone to be friendly with. So I joined the Territorial Army in Brighton and I thoroughly enjoyed that. I learned to ride a motorbike. I went scrambling and road racing. I liked riding the bike because I could be shut away, I couldn't hear anything, and I just could ride and ride. Lovely sense of freedom, and I could go fast and take risks, and it was quite exhilarating. And I suppose that was my expression, that was my freedom.

VICKY: The dice was really loaded against you, in many respects. I mean, you couldn't get a loan from a bank without a man to guarantee you. You couldn't buy anything on HP without having a man to guarantee you. I mean, a woman was definitely a second class citizen, without a doubt. They talk about inequality nowadays but you've got no real conception of what inequality was unless you lived then. We had awful trouble, Jean and I, borrowing money for a business. It was purgatory. They automatically assumed that there's always got to be a man somewhere. I mean, a salesman would come into the shop, for instance, and he would call you, 'Lovey' or 'Dearie' or 'Duckie' and, 'Where's your guv'nor, love?' I'd say, 'What do you want him for?' 'Oh, just to talk some business.' 'Well, you're talking to the owner, is that good enough for you?' But then, I'm bolshie, you see. I am that way. I mean, a man's only got to give an indication that I couldn't possibly be in charge and my back goes up a mile. But that's what it was all the time. You were fighting, all the time, because we were women in what they saw as a man's world. And to even borrow money to buy a car . . . I went into the bank to borrow money to buy a car and they said, 'Of course, you'll get your husband to sign again.' 'No, I'm not married, I'm divorced.' 'Well, haven't you got a brother or a . . .' I said, 'Why should I have anybody to guarantee me? I've got my own business, I guarantee myself.' I mean, to buy a car, Barclays Bank actually wanted me to give the deeds of my house, and I said, *'I'm only buying a car!'*

SHEILA: I would have liked to have gone into the WRNS but I was a coward and I couldn't get anybody to join with me, so the TA was the next best thing. I tried very hard to get a dispatch rider's job, but unfortunately, they didn't let women do dispatch riding, only men — mind you, they were horrible hard bikes, there was no springing, they were all rigid frames — and I kept on pestering them but no joy. They wouldn't let me do that. So I asked them if I could learn to drive. It was an MT unit, mechanical transport, it was a Royal Army Service Corps unit, we did all the transport, that was our main work to supply food and ammunition etcetera to the troops. So I learnt to drive a jeep, a Champ, a seven-ton lorry and a ten-ton lorry.

We had to learn how to repair, how to change wheels, how to change plugs. Any faults, we had to know exactly what to look for. I was coming back from Wales once, in a convoy, and my lorry broke down and I was able to diagnose what the trouble was, made a temporary repair and got all the way back to Brighton. We did quite a lot of convoy driving, most weekends, and we used to go to camp every year. I've been to Wales, Norfolk, Cornwall and most times we used to drive down in convoy. Going all round Cornwall, the roads are very narrow and we had the big troop carriers, the big ten-tonners, they were massive, great big things, you had to climb up on the wheel to get into the cab, you know, whacking great big things. And that was quite good fun because when the shops had their blinds down, and you had to go round a corner, it was sort of a fag paper between you and the blind. And the Champs used to have five forward gears and five reverse gears and in Norfolk the roads were quite long and narrow, so we used to go haring up the road, you see, slap it into reverse, into the fifth gear reverse, and then hare back all the way. And then we used to have the old-fashioned Austin ambulances and we used to do runs with those as well.

27

That was quite good fun. One day, I had a patient in the back, poor chap, he had a toothache, great big baby, and the Bognor Road ran parallel with a railway line. And there was a train going along this particular day so I decided to see if I could keep up with the train and he was in the back, yelling his head off.

I suppose in our unit half a dozen or more were gay girls. That would have been out of a couple of dozen or so.

MARGARET: I remember Vivienne saying to me, 'It's a pity we can't afford to buy a place.' So I said, 'Oh, we couldn't afford to.' It was very difficult for women to get mortgages in those days and we hadn't got any deposit or anything. Anyway, I must have spoken to my parents and my mother said, 'Well, if you ever wanted to buy a flat we could always give you some money for a deposit.' So we got one of these flats for £4,400 and we moved into that in 1963. My parents thought I was buying it on my own because my mother didn't like Vivienne, and she would never meet her. But in the end I had to, I couldn't face her, so I had to write to her that I was buying it in conjunction with my friend, Vivienne. And she wrote back and said it was a disgusting relationship that we were in, that although they had given me the deposit, they would never visit the flat while she was there.

GEORGE: When the law changed I'd been living with Steve for quite some years and it was a great sense of relief, we were now not against the law. That made a great deal of difference. We lived in flats, and I was terrified because one thing was that if you had males coming to your flat people would make comments. And you could be thrown out, they'd say there was something funny going on in there, get rid of those blokes. The reason we bought a house in the first place was that I wanted to be able to say, 'Up you!' to anyone else. No-one could tell me who could come in my house, no-one could ask me, 'What are you doing down there?' or query and question it. And I always felt vulnerable in flats, I lived in lots of flatlets, I used to smuggle people in.

I remember it was the Abbey National, I think it was, in the Western Road. And I'd got Steve in tow, he said absolutely nothing. So I said, 'Can I see the manager?' So this bloke, real bluff north country guy, he said, 'Yes.' And I said, 'Oh, I want a mortgage for myself and my friend here.' So he started to look at the form and it gave our two names, so he said, 'Mm, it's unusual to sign two men. What's going to happen if one of you decides not to pay the mortgage? How can I guarantee that there's a firm relationship there?' So I leaned across the desk, I said, 'Look, all the money we've got in the world is in my bank account. If he goes, it stays with me.' And he was good, he gave it to us. It must have been quite a thing to do then, you know.

SANDIE: I was living in Grand Parade, one of those tall houses in Grand Parade, and it was actually a house owned by a gay man and it was all converted into bedsits, except the ground floor, where he lived. He tried to get gay people if he could and there were always gay people in and out because he was very popular. And then we moved on to two rooms. I mean, that was fantastic, to have two rooms instead of one and we only had a stone sink and cold water on tap and there was a stage when there were two gay boys living on the ground floor, two gay girls living in the basement and us two on the second floor. There was a straight girl in between and an old lady in the garret at the top. But the six of us gays, we were all desperately short of money and several of us were out of work and the money just used to run out because we were all trying to help one another out and help to keep one another. And nobody minded that, of course, but we used to run out of money way in advance and so, I'm sorry to say, we took to pinching. When we were passing greengrocers' shops, where they were all out on the pavement, each one of us had to take something different, maybe your job for that day was to nab a carrot or a potato and everybody had to get something. And then into the stockpot it went and this vegetable stockpot kept us going for about three weeks at one stage. I was never so healthy and never so slim. Ah dear, it was fun. Everybody was sort of in trouble together and so nobody envied anybody or anything like that. We were just all in it together and it really was great fun and we enjoyed it.

❤   ❤   ❤

GRANT: You must remember that you had to be very discreet, you couldn't come out in the open. You had neighbours to consider, you had your families, friends, to consider, perhaps your relatives to consider. You couldn't come out of the closet. Wasn't done. It's different now, it's totally different. I mean, you can almost get up in the middle of West Street and say, 'I'm homosexual.' But you wouldn't have dared mention the word, you wouldn't have dared tell a lot of people, certainly never tell where you worked. There were a lot of elderly queans in Brighton who were comfortably off, who didn't work. Those that did were very different in their places of work, they sort of reverted to type and completely changed outside their work. You wouldn't get them swanning around in Hanningtons or anything like that. They might be serving in Hanningtons but they'd have to keep a certain amount of decorum. You didn't lisp and you didn't have broken wrists. They could fire and sack you with a week's notice, they'd only got to phone up the Labour Exchange. But if you were employed, like the majority of people, on a weekly or monthly basis, and you did something whereby the manager or the owner or the director got to hear of something that wasn't quite right, he could come in to you on a Friday, if you were paid weekly, and say, 'We shan't be needing your services any more.' Or you'd get a letter in your envelope at the end of the month saying please note that as from a certain date things have changed and you are no longer needed. Take a month's notice. You had to be very much more diplomatic. You didn't ever have to let the side down.

Sandie and girlfriend.

AILEEN: I used to sing with a country and western band and we travelled around quite a bit, and we started up a club in the Steine pub, down at the Steine. And that's where I met Lynne and Jacky. Jacky worked with horses, Lynne worked in some offices somewhere, they used to come and watch the show at the club. Afterwards I said, 'Why did you pick on me? Why did you want to get to know me?' And they said, 'Well, we knew you were gay.' I thought, 'God, what's happening?' I was picturing what I had seen of the gay life, which was these big butch numbers all dressed up, in their ties and suits, and I didn't like that. I didn't want to know that side. And I thought, 'Oh God, I hope I'm not getting to look like that.'

VALERIE: The baby butches, as we called them, were all tiny, slim little girls with short haircuts and they used to dress like boys. Now, I did find it embarrassing, if I met them in the street, because I was only three miles away from my office and occasionally, when I was out shopping, I would meet people from work. And occasionally, also, we would meet these characters and I used to be very furtive then, you know, hoping nobody from work was going to come along and see me chatting to this rather strange looking person because I was always careful about the way I appeared in public.

SHEILA: A lot of the very butch women, like Laurie for instance — she had a very good job in London, she was someone's secretary — she'd always wear collar, tie, everything masculine on top, with a skirt. So she wouldn't hide the fact of what she was. Well, she couldn't. I mean, Laurie was Laurie.

I never went to work in trousers. Well, I couldn't very well. I never wore collar and tie to work, oh, no, always open-necked and I wouldn't go out with my folks with trousers, I'd go out with a skirt.

VICKY: The first time any of my friends ever saw me in a skirt — I mean, I never thought it was ever going to happen, I never thought my two worlds would collide, but it did — I happened to have to go to work one Saturday morning and I got up, got washed and dressed and went out and I was walking down the road and all of a sudden I heard someone shout, 'Vicky!' And I thought, 'Christ, what's this?' And I turned round and there were half a dozen of my friends in a car. They were going from A to B and happened to cross my route and see me. And they said, 'Good God, we hardly recognised you!' And of course, I'd got clothes on to go to work in, which was totally different to what they'd ever seen me in. It was a laugh for a few minutes but I think I nearly died. Yes, I was embarrassed. Very much so. I think the only people that ever got away with it, a very popular job at the time, was working in petrol stations. They never wore a collar and tie but they certainly went to work looking butch and they stood out like a sore thumb, you know. I mean, you pulled in — there was no unmanned petrol stations then — and nearly every garage you pulled into, there'd be a girl working there somewhere, you'd see a girl and she stood out as butch a mile away. But I should think that, even then, they looked so butch that, most of the time, people would think they were boys.

GERALD: One had to . . . not expose it. There were employers who simply did not and would not tolerate known gay employees; and people were frightened of losing their jobs, especially if they were apprehended by the police on even a minor gay charge. Once it hit the media, there was always

Top left Vera at Contours
Travel Agents.
Top centre Kay at her desk.
Above Janine when she was
a hospital administrator.
Far left Bobby and some of
her early work.
Left Helen waiting for the
football results to phone to her
newsdesk.

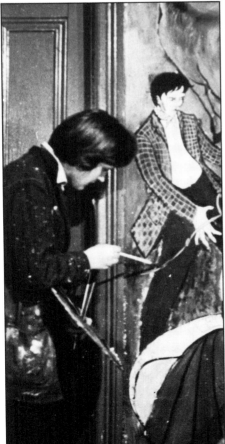

somebody in the firm who was willing to send it anonymously in an envelope to one of the directors; and people were much more in fear of their careers in those days. It is a thousand pities that since the consenting adults act came in, that all the ground had been made, a great proportion of it has been lost through this wretched and horrific AIDS. That is the saddest thing of all. It's the worst thing, certainly, that's ever happened in my life.

GILL: I must have been about nineteen, coming along for twenty. I joined the police force. I went away, you have to go and do thirteen weeks basic training. The day we arrived we were shown to our room and I went in and deposited my luggage and there wasn't anyone in there. We went to this sort of meeting place, where we were introduced to our room mates and, of all the women that I was in with, I think the only other lesbian on the course, she and I were in the same room. I don't think I formed an immediate attraction but it grew very quickly and it wasn't long before we were experiencing this lust for each other and I can't explain, I mean, how do you know that you're attracted to someone, how do you know that this feeling that's building up between, it's just like a magnet, isn't it? But there's some feeling there. And so one night we were watching a film show on the camp and we suddenly found that we were holding hands underneath our arms and so when we left there we raced back to our room and there was a passionate embrace and hey ho away we go!

Well, we were both investigated by the CID because someone reported us for having unnatural desires on each other and behaving like cows in a field, was the way they put it. I said to Molly that we must deny it all the way, on no account are we to admit to anything and she went along with that. We were both interviewed separately and they used every trick in the book to try and trick us into admitting what we'd done, saying that one of us had said something when we hadn't. That's the usual way that the police operate. We just denied everything.

GERALD: They certainly wouldn't have dared be camp in business 'cause they would simply have been dismissed. It was not illegal to dismiss somebody, and without giving a reason. And they had to go! They took whatever holiday money was due to them and that was it. And their card was stamped and they were given their P45 and out the door — within an hour! Things were very different. And people were much more concerned about not losing their positions. And perhaps they did go out at night into the bars and whoop it up a bit as a release yeah. Perhaps it is so.

JAMES: People would try desperately to keep their private life and work life well apart, to an extent that's barely needed these days. Probably teaching or some other sensitive area would be the only one, these days, where one would still have to be a bit cautious but in those days the two things were kept totally separate, for safety. Most work employers would certainly sack you, if you were caught cottaging or something like that but I think a lot of employers would have sacked people for having discovered they were gay, frankly. Dressmakers or something of that sort, where it might be expected, something arty, theatrical but most ordinary employers would consider it unacceptable or somehow it would be that one's fellow workers would be in moral risk or some moral danger.

JOCELYN: They accepted gay men in the theatre, yes — they were rather a fun joke — and they were all so nice and such fun. But when I was in the theatre I didn't ever come across any comments about gay women. If so, I think they would be fairly derogatory, 'Oh, *she's* a lesbian.' They weren't accepted in the same way that gay men were, as being fun. I think they were thought to be rather dreary.

AILEEN: Harriet went to work on the buses. I lived in Church Road, Hove, and there was a bus stop just facing the kitchen window and she'd phone me up and she'd say, 'I'm passing by at such and such a time, watch out for me.' And she'd pass by and suddenly the back door of the bus would fly open. She'd be there, waving away. Couldn't *believe* it! And, of course, everybody on the bus would be looking. Ah dear, it was so funny. And I'd be hiding behind the curtains.

JAMES: I can remember with my boss one day walking through Ship Street and a character, Michael, The Duchess of Argyle, went by wearing heavy colouring on his face. Michael was very discreet and didn't nod or anything as he passed by. We were actually frightened, you see, of recognition from someone like that in those days 'cause it could mean loss of job, and unemployment was a real threat. And this lad didn't show the least bit of recognition, not even half a wink or a nod. And my boss, who was sort of liberal minded, had noticed this character go by with the slap on and said, 'Well, I suppose he can't help his make-up.' And I said, 'No, but he needn't wear it.' And that got over that. Whether my boss suspected anything I don't know, really don't know.

AILEEN: I found out one other chap in the grocery trade that we were in, he was married and he was having a terrible time. And he started speaking to me and he says, 'I need somebody to come with me to this pub.' And he mentioned a pub, Spotted Dog. And I said yes, I'd been there before. And he says, 'You're not gay, are you?' and I says, 'Yes,' and I blushed like hell. So I says, 'Why do you want to go there?' And he mentioned he had met somebody but he didn't have the guts to go there on his own. He was rather embarrassed about it. Would I go with him? So I says, 'Yes.' So every dinner time we'd go down there. Now the rumour worked round like wild fire that we were having a wild love affair and even his wife came to see me about this. And I says, 'Well, I'm terribly sorry but if he hasn't got the guts to tell you, I will.' Well, she couldn't believe it. And anyway Frank saw me about the next day and he says, 'You did something I never had the guts to do.' He says, 'And it's given me the opportunity to move out.' So he did. And he moved in with his boyfriend.

❤   ❤   ❤

HELEN: All I know is that anonymous letters had turned up at the paper I worked on, saying that I was a lesbian and that I was a nasty piece of work and I was breaking people's hearts and didn't care what I did and that sort of thing. My mother got one and said, 'What does this mean?' 'Well,' I said, 'I think it means that I like women, mum.' And she said, 'Well,

> "You lived in a cocoon because you couldn't tell anybody. I mean nobody knew at work, when I was going out to work. You had to live a sort of fictional life because you couldn't talk about it. VICKY"

33

so do I.' And I said, 'Well, of course we do,' and sort of tossed it off. But these letters went round, which was most embarrassing. I was terribly worried about it. I mean, there is nothing nastier.

BUCK: When I was demobbed from the army I got my first job as a manager in the restaurant world. Well, you obviously pick up people and they knew that you were in a good position and, of course, in those days it was *verboten* to be queer. They would hold that over you, and of course, I was handling lots of money at the time and it would be just twenty pounds here and there . . . the mistake was ever giving in once. What I should have done, but you wouldn't dare, is turn round and say, 'Go to hell.' But then it would go from twenty to fifty and then a bottle of scotch here or a bottle of gin there until it really got out of hand. You had to do something about it so you would get your gay friends together and somebody always knew some heavy guy. But that was trying. It was so easy because it was so underground that they had this power, they had this power over you.

SANDIE: I had been to teacher training college in Birmingham, where I met a girl who was six months younger than I was — I'd just turned my twenty-first birthday — and she told her parents that we were gay. They got me kicked out of training college. They said, if I ever saw their daughter again, they'd have me through court. So I left training college and went to work in various factories.

Teaching was all I ever really wanted to do. So, three years after I moved to Brighton, I wrote round every single private school in Brighton and Hove and one accepted me as a supply teacher. I did that for two years, that was juniors. I've still got a reference from that school, wonderful reference; the headmaster gave me a superb reference, so I suppose I must have done well enough there.

But then, because I wasn't fully qualified, you could only do two years supply teaching, so I applied to go back to college in Bognor Regis. I went along for the interview and the interview went well and I was so sure that I'd got a place because the principal came running down the road after me and said, 'By the way, if I can't find you a place on the college campus, are you prepared to live out?' I said, 'Yes, of course I will.' And I went back home to my girlfriend and said, 'Great, I'm in. I must be. He wouldn't have said that otherwise.' And yet a fortnight later, back came a letter saying that I hadn't been accepted. And of course, when I thought about it I realised there's a clearing house in London for teachers and my file must have had lesbian stamped all over it, so that was that. I knew I would never get into teaching then, so I didn't try again. It really messed my life up. I felt there wasn't anything else I could really do well.

GILL: When I joined the army I was quite sorry for myself. This particular woman stayed behind one night in the barracks and I started talking to her. I told her how I felt about women or how I thought I felt. I didn't know but I was saying that I had this very strange feeling towards women. I said I almost feel that I could kill the woman. I didn't really know what this feeling was that I was experiencing. And, of course, she completely flipped, me saying this, and she suddenly rushed into the corner and tried to get away from me. And she was screaming and carrying on and, of course, reported me to the corporal in charge and I was in front of the M.O. and told that I would be seen by a psychiatrist and would possibly be out of the army — which I was in very quick time. On my discharge papers it said that I had a psychopathic personality, whatever that means, I don't know. But when I went to see the psychiatrist to tell him all about my life and what I felt for women he assured me that I was a perfectly healthy woman. He asked me if I thought I wanted to be a man and I didn't. But I couldn't understand why I didn't want to be a man. Anyway he eventually discharged me after quite a number of visits and told me that I was a perfectly normal young lady, that I should go away and get myself a boyfriend, get married and have children and live happily ever after. I said, 'Thank you very much, doctor, I'm cured!' And here I am.

JANICE: When I was twenty, I actually had a nervous breakdown because of pressure and all sorts of things. I ended up going into Graylingwell, which was a very prominent nuthouse down in Chichester at the time. I had agoraphobia, that's what form the breakdown took, and I was really bad with it. I couldn't walk from one room to another. Anyway, I went into the mental hospital a total wreck, but pleased to be there because anything to get away from home would have been wonderful. All the women there were very nice to me and they said, 'You've got to keep away from this woman called Stella, you must keep away from her.' I said, 'Well, why?' Now Stella was a very attractive thirty year old, very old I thought, very pretty, married with two children. They would say, 'Keep away from her 'cause she likes young girls.' Well, I tell you what, I have never manipulated things so much in all my life. I thought, 'This has got to be it now.' Ill as I was, I thought, 'I've got to get in tow with this Stella, I've got to start talking to her.' And I did just that. A lot of people used to go home at weekends there because nobody was ill to the point of being physically violent or anything like that — we were all just doped up to the eyeballs — and Stella actually made a pass at me finally. I'd never felt so happy and elated in all my life. This is what I'd been looking for, this was it, this was the missing piece of the puzzle and my health improved dramatically, oh, yes, very much so, it definitely did, I never looked back really.

I did see a psychiatrist, obviously, as everyone did while you were there and I told the psychiatrist of my feelings about this and I am very, very angry to this day about that. I was under twenty-one then and the age of consent for anything was twenty-one and the actual psychiatrists had to see your parents in those days, if you were in hospital like that. And they told them, the psychiatrist told my parents about me being lesbian and this resulted in me being forced, against my will, to have aversion treatment in the hospital, which to this day I will never forgive them for. It was appalling to have to go through something like that. The treatment went over six weeks and the idea is you are given injections and made to feel physically ill at the sight of women doing anything. For about three months I felt dreadful about it, I mean, I couldn't face being anywhere near the proximity

> **"**I had a lot of pressure when people knew I was gay. I got a lot of advice from doctors in the family like, 'You just need to spend one night with a good man, my dear, and you'll be alright.' I mean they really did believe that.
> JANINE **"**

of women. But what it doesn't do, you see, is make you like men any more. It can't actually make you like something. It can put you off something you do like but it certainly can't work the other way round. So, poor Stella, I mean, once the hospital realised what was happening, we were separated at the speed of light and Stella was then discharged. But it didn't stop it really, because all it did, once the treatment wore off, I'd learnt to be crafty. I no longer told the truth in these sessions. I said what they wanted me to say, really, in order to get better, in order to get out and see her. So, in actual fact, she instigated my recovery quite a lot, without realising it.

I stayed in touch with Stella even though she had been discharged from Graylingwell. Illicit phone calls and coded letters and all sorts, yes. She used to write to me and call herself the Reverend Newstead. 'Cause all your letters were read just in case, you know. I suppose it was a bit like being in prison really.

Fortunately I haven't had a nervous breakdown since and I haven't had to go back anywhere like this, but I know that when I left there, I was still a wreck. You don't get over these things in five minutes, it took about three years, I suppose. And one of the psychiatrists I saw after that said the only way you'll ever get better is to live the sort of life you need to live. You can't be so restrained and bottle things up the way you are. And I mean it wasn't as if I was a child molester or something. But you were then, in fact, put in the same category.

GEORGE: At one point in my life, I decided I wasn't going to be gay. And I wasn't going to be straight, there was no question of that. I was not going to be anything, I was going to be a bookworm, a sitter-in listening to music, going to the theatre and the cinema. I would avoid all gay friends and I would avoid all straight friends. And so I spent a period, I can't tell you what sort of time, totally alone. I would come home from work, in a flat that I had in Hove or wherever I was at the time, cook my meal and spend the evening listening to the radio or reading books. If people rang me up at work to go out I would always put them off, say, 'No.' And I can remember on a Sunday, for example, I'd be so bored I'd just walk around the square a couple of times and then come back in again.

BUCK: I came down to Brighton. I went to work at Clarges hotel, as a trainee receptionist, where I stayed seventeen years and finished up marrying the governor which causes much laughter amongst most of my friends. In fact I was married three times. Every time I got lonely, I got married. I'm not sure whether it's the bouquet or the white dress, but none of them lasted very long. I think it was out of sheer loneliness. Loneliness is the worst ship that ever set to sea. Terrible.

SIOBHAN: Certainly I've been aware over the years of attempted suicides and I've attempted suicide several times. It was part of the stresses that I knew in my life and in other people's lives around me at the time. Certainly part of that was to do with being lesbian, the isolation. I wasn't conforming to any heterosexual role.

GRANT: People were far more anti-queer in the fifties and sixties than they are now. They didn't accept it. They don't accept it wholeheartedly now but then it wasn't accepted in any way. I mean people, boys and girls, when they were proved to be queer, have committed suicide because they couldn't tell their parents. Or they would leave home and disappear. They were too ashamed. There was a completely different attitude. They were in the closet, they were certainly not coming out.

JANICE: I had a very bad time when one relationship ended, I decided I'd try having a boyfriend again because I felt very, very insecure. I was one of these dumb twits that believe, as people still do, that getting married might have been a salvation in that at least they'd have some form of security, which of course is total bullshit but at that time I believed it. So I had a couple of boyfriends but it was pointless really. I had a lot of pressure from my mother as well, I mean, the whole idea of me being gay was just appalling.

JOHN: In my early days I used to prefer men much older than myself. There was the famous showbiz lawyer, David Jacobs, he was my lover. He was found hanged in his garage. Nobody ever knew why, I still to this day can't decide. Some people say that he committed suicide. Some people say that the mafia did him in. But he was just found hanging there by one of his servants, luckily not by me, and I only heard about it when I saw it in the newspapers. It was a terrible thing to read in a newspaper that your lover was found hanging and nobody had bothered to tell you. Not even his servants bothered to phone me.

GEORGE: This is a true story to show you what I mean about fear. When Steve moved into Sackville Gardens in Hove I decided to go and sleep the Saturday night there with him. Now I went in there very late at night so nobody would see me come in but during the night unfortunately it snowed really heavily, really heavily, so then when you got to the front door it was pristine, okay, and there was no way I could go out of that door in case anyone saw me and those footsteps would show he'd had someone in his room for the night. So I stayed there till three in the afternoon until they cleared it and they'd all gone and I snuck out.

JOCELYN: Well, I knew I couldn't tell the whole world because of her inhibitions and because of my husband. And I didn't really want to tell. I couldn't have just gone to him and said, 'Look here, old boy, I'm afraid I'm gay.' You know: 'I don't mind going on living with you but I'm going to be having affairs with women,' which in today's climate one might do, but in those days it was the 1950s and you just didn't talk about it.

PETER: It was part of the excitement, was the secrecy. It was all hush-hush and there was a certain amount of suave in it, in those days, which there isn't now, it's lost. The queans these days, they go camping it around quite openly and it's lost something. It's lost a bit of its charm about it, the fact that it's no longer a secret. Now you're gay or you're straight, you're one or the other. It's lost a certain of its colour for the fact that it's no longer slightly underground.

> 66 I mustn't let you think that we ran around with false moustaches and beards and dark glasses, dead scared and frightened, thinking are the police going to pick me up at any minute. Some people did, some people were absolutely terrified of someone saying something out of place . . . and some folk still are I suppose.
> JAMES 99

VICKY: It was a very insular position really because you became part of a very close-knit family, if you like. And the outside world didn't really encroach on it. And if you didn't go looking for trouble, trouble didn't find you. I mean, you didn't go out blazoning the fact. If you went anywhere, you went by taxi. You didn't walk on the streets dressed like we used to dress, for instance. If you couldn't get in a car or get a taxi, then you didn't go.

GEORGE: I had friends who didn't even know my real name. I can only speak for me, I can't say that everyone else was like me, I think a lot of us were. But certainly you never discussed where you worked, you never gave your real name, you'd be Bill or Harry. I had some friends in Hove, and I used to socialise with them but it was very difficult for me because I thought some of them were pretty careless in their relationships and I always thought that if one gets caught, they'll all get caught. And if they've got your telephone number . . . I lived in terror. But, as I say, that's the way I felt, I can't say how others felt, I never really discussed it with any of them, but I was terrified of the law, terrified of them.

♥   ♥   ♥

DENNIS: I never really had a steady affair, certainly not at that stage in my life. I didn't like the idea of an affair. I don't think it was safe to have an affair anyway. It was really causing trouble. You had to be terribly, terribly, terribly careful if you did have an affair. I'll give you a case in point. While I was in the army, I met a quean, well, I couldn't help but meet her, called Percy. Well, he had an affair, I think it was 1957 when it all blew up, anyway he had an affair, who was about his own age. They'd been going out together for about two years and Percy was at work one day and his father went into his bedroom and went rooting round in Percy's drawers and found this letter. Well, I don't know what was in the letter but father read the letter and went to the police with it, you see, so they arrested him at work, they arrested the boyfriend at his work as well, took them both to the station and did the usual thing, keeping them in separate rooms and not letting them see one another, for about five hours, came and said, 'Right. Well, your mate's confessed everything so you may as well confess as well and it'll make it a lot easier because then you'll get off light.' So thereupon Percy told them everything that they wanted to know and then, armed with this, they went back and got a statement out of the boyfriend because he hadn't confessed at all. Typical, nasty, fuzz trick. Anyway the upshot of it all was that they both got three years in prison simply on the strength of a letter that one had written the other; and it ruined Percy's life, he never really recovered; and this happened to so many people.

So it was quite dangerous to have an affair, you know, and all the time I was coming down to Brighton I never kept the names and addresses of Brighton friends written down, it was in my head but I never wrote it down on anything and I would certainly never dream of keeping a diary because I knew loads and loads and loads of queans who were arrested and then they'd go to their house and go through their rooms and they'd find a diary and they'd go through names in that and it could snowball. It was a terrifying thing. I always thought it wasn't safe to have affairs. One night

Top left Bob and Harry, the Bookends.
Left Bob and Harry at a beatnik party.
Top right Buck with poodle, Tio.
Above Peter at a formal dinner.

> **❝** When I was first seeing Bob he had an old Ford that you had to keep pulling the choke out every time you went round a corner. Never mind, there wasn't very many cars about. There wasn't the money. I thought it was very grand having a boyfriend with a car! HARRY **❞**

stands with somebody whose name you didn't know and certainly whose address you didn't know and they didn't know yours was really a much better idea. And I think really that's true, it's probably why I got away with it all those years.

RICHARD: It sounds as if I had lots of affairs, but they were mismatches really, and very abusive. It always made me wonder whether I was being punished for being what I was. 'It can't be right otherwise it would work,' sort of thing. That was another thing that I had to try and deal with. I realise that's total nonsense now but it certainly wasn't then, it was very difficult. I used to lie awake nights worrying about what I was into. Whenever anything went wrong and I got these people into my life, it was like someone slapping me and saying, 'You shouldn't be doing this. You're going to get hurt.'

PETER: It's a lonely scene the gay scene, extremely lonely. If you like your own company, you have enough intelligence to cope with your own company, then you're alright, but I know a lot of people that didn't, and I've known a couple that have committed suicide because they couldn't cope with it. Everybody in the gay scene, I suppose, they all seem to be searching, searching and looking. Affairs never seem to last very long, perhaps they didn't in those days. I've been one of the lucky ones, tied them down to the bedpost, made sure they didn't get away. But I've had a long-standing affair with Ted. When I first knew him, he was nineteen, I was a chicken-snatcher you see. But now it's something more than an affair. It's not a sexual relationship we have, it's something above that, it's something more golden, we've been together a long time. It's part of me now. But these people in the gay crowd, they seemed to find someone and it was, 'Oh! It's marvellous, I'm in love, darling!' And the next couple of weeks they'd've forgotten even his name. 'Oh, her. I never see her now, dear.'

Eddie.

ERIC: His name was Eddie. I met him at the dog-track in Hove. He was from Dublin and he used to sing in Chatfield's. He had a good voice and he used to sing 'Danny Boy' and all the old queans would start crying into their gin. We lived in Clarendon Road which is now Churchill Square, I had a bedsitter upstairs and he had a bedsitter down below. He was mad about a woman who was much older than himself, who was a manageress of one of the hotels, but he was partly rent — he would expect you to give him something — and so we used to have sex together on that understanding. Then sometimes he would arrive home at two o'clock in the morning and wake me up and say, 'Come on, I'm hungry, I want you to cook me something.' That meant egg and chips or something like that and he said, 'If you don't do it quickly I'm going to burn your curtains down.' He would hold his lighter, or throw your transistor out of the window, things like that. I suppose I really loved him in a way.

HARRY: How did I meet Bob? That'd be saying! In the usual place! The very famous cottage down Black Lion Street. We met in there in 1959. It's not there now. It was a great big long one, with all stalls all one side.

40

He was at one end and I was at the other. And there was several others in the middle. We sort of made eye contact right down the room! That's how we met.

It wasn't love at first sight, I don't think you could say that. No, I think we sort of grew into it because, I mean, Bob was still at home and I was still with my old school pal in our flat in Vernon Terrace. We became attached to each other very gradually, it wasn't one of those overnight falling affairs and I think that's probably why, although we're sort of not a pair any more in the usual sense, we're still together. We grew into it and we've grown into each other instead of a wild passionate affair sort of thing. Though the other thing is that we've always shared everything. We've always shared our home, shared our money and everything. Everything.

ANNIE: Katie came down with me and then eventually she wanted to buy a house, she wanted to come in with me. In other words, get more kind of clamped on to me. Financially as well, you see. So I gave in, again, and said 'Okay, we'll get a bigger house.' So we moved and got a bigger house. And I think our relationship really wasn't very good at that time. In a way, I suppose, we were, sort of, married, because she would go out to work, and I would be doing the housework and the gardening most of the time. Which rather annoyed me. It used to get me down because I felt I was doing all the chores. She wasn't very good at it. And she drove me nearly potty because she would have the television on, all the time, and always things I didn't want to look at. I remember having to sit through hours and hours and hours of stuff like Coronation Street. And I began to get more and more frustrated and desperate, you know. Didn't know how to get out of it. Because we hadn't got a lot in common, I'm afraid. But we'd been together such a long time and it was becoming such a habit. She was so determined to make it a permanent thing. I suppose I probably initiated most of the sex side of it. But then we didn't really have an awful lot of sex by that time. We had separate rooms, I don't think we often slept together then. We were more like Darby and Joan, I think, than anything else.

GILL: Jess worked in a factory. She was very butch-looking. She had her hair swept back. She didn't have it cropped but she used to sweep it back. She always wore a man's shirt and tailored skirt. She'd had smallpox when she was a child and it had left her very pockmarked and so she wore a lot of this pan-stick that made her look as if she'd got a mask on.

The second time I went into Pigott's, Jess came in and that was the next thirteen years of my life taken care of. She came in and said, 'Hello, would you like a drink?' so I said, 'Yes, please.' So she bought me a drink and asked me what I was doing and who I was with and, 'Have you got anyone?' I said, 'No.' I don't know at what point she said, 'Well, you're mine now.' She took me down onto the seafront and I was absolutely terrified of being with her 'cause I thought she was going to grab me and take me onto the pebbles and rape me and do all sorts. I was really quite frightened. I think she did eventually kiss me somewhere along the seafront. I was desperately lonely and I wanted someone and I grabbed at the first straw. I'd been on my own for what seemed like so many years that the first person that showed a scrap of warmth towards me, I was theirs.

> 66 I think there were a few lesbian couples that I knew where one had children from a previous marriage that was brought up as a family. But they always lived in bloody awful fear of anybody, of the father finding out that the woman was a lesbian because I think it was always thought that the children would be taken away. VICKY 99

I knew it was wrong from the word go, it just didn't feel right at all, the whole thing. She was about twenty years older than me and we weren't really socially compatible, but she took me over, yes, she totally took me over. So I was play-acting, really, because I'd decided that I was going to be fem and she decided that she was going to marry me and be my husband. I had to be totally hers. My life was bed — to sleep — and going to bingo 'cause she used to like playing bingo, so we used to do that nearly every night. Whilst I was with her I had one or two affairs and she found out about them. She never hit me but I felt she could. I had an affair with one of the usherettes at the Savoy cinema — it's the Cannon now — and she went down and sorted her out at the cinema. Called her a Judas and how dare she try and take her friend away. She nearly got her the sack.

HARRIET: Bill. I don't know why she was called Bill 'cause she was very feminine. I was waiting hopefully for Bill all my life, probably. She was an absolutely magnificent creature, she was gorgeous, lovely Siamese eyes, slanting and blue, naturally turned-up nose, gorgeous voice, lovely, happy — some people's voices are gloriously happy and she'd got one of them. She just sort of said, 'I'm not as other women . . .' All sorts of things, delightful things. The point was, she was devoted to this wretched old woman, Sylvia, she was . . . oh, I suppose she must have been years older, she must have been about seventies or eighties when I was still in the thirties, and she would never admit it, she always said she was Bill's aunt, you know aunt and niece and nothing in the world would shake them from that. I adored her, absolutely worshipped her. Eventually I was getting so upset because I couldn't really get anywhere with her — I mean, she encouraged me, she gave me her love and her friendship and all that — but eventually, I wanted to get away. I knew that Harold could, would stop me, 'cause he was a very strong-willed man, he was the only person that could stop me, he controlled me more than anybody else I knew. So I married him.

Kay Dick.

GERALD: I had various affairs. I think I had six people I was in love with . . . The longest relationship I had went on for about seven and a half years, and the shortest one, just a few months. But I've never been one of these people to be off with the old and on with the new all the time, because I think, if you do that, it merely blunts your emotions, and I think that's dangerous. I've always thought that a one to one relationship is ideal — long, long, long before this horrible Acquired Immune Deficiency Syndrome came on the scene. It was always much nicer to be with somebody, and not only that, it looked very odd, if you were always seen in the company of different young men! When you were seen out in the town. But if you were seen out with a particular friend, then that was much more acceptable.

BUCK: I think the longest affair lasted about a year, two possibly. Unfortunately he was an alcoholic, loved him very much, but the drink came between us in the end. It nearly killed me and I nearly killed him.

I've got a lot of friends that have been living together for forty or fifty odd years and they still love each other. That's what I always wanted and was never able to attain.

AILEEN: Well, first time I met Harriet, I was working for a company called Trident, which dealt with vacuum cleaners. I was told by one of the managers there was this lady downstairs, looked like a butch number. There was about two of us went down to have a look at this butch number. Anyway, her name was Harriet. She came onto the team and we started doing calls round places and the first encounter I had with Harriet, she was doing a demonstration of this hoover. And what happened was, instead of having the suction going, she had the blowing-out going, so all this dust was flying out all over the place! So that was my first encounter and I thought, 'God, what have they brought on here!'

At that time, I was living with my sister down Fourth Avenue and not much money, 'cause sales weren't that good on the machines and Harriet noticed this and she would be buying double sandwiches and saying, 'Have a sandwich.' You know, 'Come on, have a sandwich.' And I thought, 'Awfully kind . . .' We got to know one another and got on okay. There was one other girl which I thought Harriet was after.

Anyway, the two of us decided we felt sorry for Harriet, all by herself with her books, so we'd go round and see her. My God, chase me Charlie! I got the shock of my life, 'cause I thought it was the other girl that Harriet was after and suddenly I found that it *wasn't* the other girl that Harriet was after and that put the fear of death into me because at that time I didn't realise I was gay. As far as I was concerned, my fate in life was going to be a married woman with a family and, at that time, I was going quite strongly with a chap anyway.

I think it was more curiosity than anything else, I kept going back to see Harriet. I got to like her but I was still terribly unsure. *Eventually*, there was one night I went round to Harriet's, she'd invited me round for a meal. I went round to the place, and I'd never had a meal like it . . .

HARRIET: Sirloin steaks or something . . .

AILEEN: You gave me sauerkraut. I'll never forget it. 'Cause I'd never had it before and I didn't know what to expect. Anyway, we got chatting away, we got talking to one another. Harriet walked me home, and I walked Harriet home, and Harriet walked me back home. A couple of hours passed before we decided, right, that was enough. Nothing had happened in between that.

I was terribly frightened, I didn't know what was going on. I was very unsure, I couldn't make out what was happening to me, so I decided that was it, I didn't want to see her. I was fighting against it. And I concentrated on Stuart, who I was going out with at that time. And then I got this nasty little letter . . .

HARRIET: It was a brilliant letter! It wasn't a *nasty* little letter.

AILEEN: . . . which put the fear of God into me. As far as I could read, she was going to commit suicide because I wasn't going round to see her . . .

HARRIET: Took me *hours* to compose.

AILEEN: . . . and I thought, 'God!' and went dashing round there. And there she was, quite happily sitting there, reading a book. I could have killed her, 'cause I'd imagined everything that was going to happen. And that very

66 When we broke up, which you can read about in 'The Shelf', I remained in Hampstead for five years and so did she. As soon as I moved to Brighton, madam sold her place up. There's a wonderful thing that Jane Carlyle said to Thomas Carlyle one day; she said to him, 'If I should leave you today, I would have to come back tomorrow to see how you were getting on without me.' And now Sarah lives round the corner. KAY 99

night was the final night. I realised then . . . I stayed the night with her. It was a lovely feeling, just being together. I still wasn't quite sure what was happening. I was still fighting it. Again, I sort of didn't want to see her. There were phone calls . . . flowers . . .

HARRIET: Which she gave to her mother.

AILEEN: . . . which I gave to my mother, I didn't want to know.

HARRIET: I was *outraged*, out of season too!

AILEEN: I kept putting Harriet off, I didn't want to see her and it went on for quite a while. She kept coming round, climbing up the drainpipe . . .

HARRIET: Age of forty-two or something dreadful!

AILEEN: I couldn't believe it. This face appeared in the window. I thought, 'My God!'

HARRIET: I wasn't going to be defeated! I was quite frantic, quite annoyed. It was, '*Does* she like me? *Doesn't* she?' You know, just the usual old thing. I was determined to rescue her from these wretched men.

AILEEN: The decision came when something happened in my home, with my mother and sister, and I packed my bags and I went round to Harriet. On the doorstep, knocked on the door and said, 'Right. I've come to live with you.' Shock. She didn't expect it.

It was beautiful, the way our sexual relationship developed. It was left for me to make the move. We used to cuddle one another. But one morning when we woke up and I turned round and looked at her, that, that was it. There's nothing . . . you can't explain that feeling. It's what had been there for years, waiting to come out, suddenly came out and went to the right person. How I felt afterwards, I was all mixed up, I didn't know how I felt, but I knew if we got some place of our own, it would be alright. So, we set up in our furnished accommodation and it was lovely; lovely place it was. And even then, the chap that I used to go with still kept coming round and in the latter end he turned round and said that was it. He could fight a man but he couldn't fight the woman, which was Harriet. And when he said that, he asked me to make the decision. And I don't know why but I made the decision to live with Harriet.

GEORGE: One Sunday, two heterosexual friends of mine took me down to Chatfield's, and suddenly, across the room, I saw this guy, which was Steve, and I thought, 'Oh, I know him from Shoreham, seen him.' And I quite liked the look of him, he looked quite nice and gentle and smiled and acknowledged me, and I smiled. So, the following day, I went into Shoreham and I walked into the shop where he worked and I didn't know what to do, because suddenly I'm in the International Stores and I thought, 'What am I going to do with this man, what am I going to say to him, for Christ's sake?' So I hung around looking, because they used to serve you in those days, it wasn't self-service like it is now. Finally, he came in my direction. I said, 'Can I have a half-pound of ginger nuts, please?' That was all I could think of to say. So he goes and gets me this half-pound of ginger nuts, and he's looking furtively about him, and I'm looking about and he said, 'I saw you in Chatfield's the other night,' you know, look, look. And he said he went

Left Vera, Jo and two queer friends on Palace Pier, coming over normal.
Below Vera, Margaret and her grandson.

6362

45

into a bar called the Argyle, and I said, 'Oh, I go there.' I didn't even know where it was! I said, 'I go there,' you see, so he said, 'Oh, I'll meet you in there next Saturday night.' So I thought, 'Oh, I'll go in there and have some of this!' Grabbed my ginger nuts, and ran.

So I go down to Brighton on Saturday night and I ask someone where the Argyle is and they said, 'Oh, it's in Middle Street.' So I bowled into this bar, and I didn't know it was a cocktail bar only, and this twinkling piano in the corner, and it was all very genteel and there was a lady with a deaf-aid, wonderful woman, behind the bar, and I bowled in there and said, 'Brown ale, please,' and the place went quiet. She said, 'We don't sell brown ale, this is a cocktail bar.' And I'm sort of saying, 'What's a cocktail, can I have one?'

I knew I liked him; I don't know why I liked him, but I did like him. And it sounds like Mills and bleeding Boon, really, but one night we walked out of the Argyle bar and walked all the way home along the seafront. It was February, must have been off our bleeding trolley; February, it was covered in snow, and we sat in one of those booths down there. We didn't do anything physically or sexually or anything like that, I mean, we kissed and cuddled for about three and a half hours. It never happened to me before, I'd never kissed anyone like that before, never kissed anyone like that. I didn't want it to stop, it just went on and on and on and on, and he felt the same. And we just knew that something had to happen, and funnily enough I didn't care who knew, it didn't matter any more, I'd got somebody who cared about me.

Seafront shelter.

BOBBY: This friend of mine with whom I now live was another teacher on the staff and I felt very wary about making any approaches to her because I didn't want to spoil the friendship and so it took me a good three months before I tentatively mentioned about it. She had no experience whatsoever of any emotional partnerships, certainly she hadn't had any sexual experience at all, which is unusual because she was about twenty-five by then. She told me then that she'd had various feelings but she didn't know what they were, she didn't know how to define them or categorise them. She was obviously interested because she kept on inviting me to go to theatre or go out to places and I was resisting like hell all the time. I felt that she might not approve of it. That's going back to another experience I'd had, of trusting people and telling them things and then they went mad and berserk and over the top, so I was very, very cautious about it. And, eventually, I made up my mind it was very simple just to try and get closer, that was alright.

I was in my landlady's house, I had taken a room in a house belonging to some very interesting and rather eccentric people that had four children. And my friend, Sandra, with whom I had become friendly at school, she was directing the school plays and things, and I was doing the scenery and what not, and my landlady said, 'Bring your friends back whenever you want to.' And so I did invite her home for meals and things sometimes. Eventually I managed a situation where she had to stay the night. It was my landlady's wedding anniversary and I think it was a Saturday night or something and we'd been rehearsing the kids at school all day and I said to Ruth, my landlady, 'I will cook for you and Tony tonight, I'll do you a meal.' So I invited Sandra and a couple of other people and cooked a meal for them all and said to Sandra, 'Stay. You know you don't have to go home, you can stay.' And Ruth had set up the guest bedroom for her. They didn't care a hoot, these people; they were very urbane and very sophisticated. Quite well off background they came from, you know, upper middle class, so they didn't care a damn. I'm sure they knew exactly what was going on.

Well, when we'd finished the meal with Ruth and Tony and everybody else, and the others had gone home, I said to Sandra, 'Do you want to come upstairs to my little garret for a final cup of coffee?' All very pure in those days, hardly used to drink or anything. So she said, 'Yes.' So she came up. We were having our final cup of coffee and I said to her, 'Go to the window and look outside at the moon, it's wonderful.' So she went to the window and looked at the moon and I went up beside her and got up as close as I could, without being too awful, and I just sort of put my head on her shoulder and said, 'Isn't it beautiful and romantic?' I think she kissed me at that point and I thought, 'Oh, good, I've got a chance now.' So I kissed her more . . . better and then I said, 'Take your clothes off if you want to.' So there we were. She took her clothes off and popped into my tiny little single bed and that was our first encounter. Meanwhile, the guest bedroom had been prepared for her downstairs in the house and the fire had been put on and the hot water bottle had been put in the bed, so about six o'clock in the morning I said, 'Don't you think you ought to go down to the guest bedroom?' And she, bless her heart, said, 'No, I'm not going to pretend any more.'

It was very serious, it was very profound . . . and has been for twenty-five years, a very profound relationship. I have always felt that she's not really a lesbian but she has always felt that she's not really a heterosexual either. I suppose my Catholic self was saying the right thing will happen, she will meet a nice man and get married and settle down and have a family.

H ENRY: I got fed up with the local pubs and I met a chap one day and he said, 'Come and join the clubs.' I was a member at the Queen of Clubs for quite a long time and one day Phil said to me, 'He's a nice boy and he's keen on you, this one who comes in latish on a Saturday night, I'll fix it up for you.' So I said, 'Alright.' So, anyway, he came over, put a couple of drinks on the table where I was sitting and said, 'Have you got a flat?' I said, 'Yes.' So he said, 'Would you like me to take you round there, I'd like to go.' And he had a shower, and when he came in, in my dressing gown, he'd got such a beautiful body, and he was slightly ginger with freckles — quite attractive they are, those gingery, freckly boys. So he let me play with him and I played with him and in the end I said, 'Oh! get into bed.' Anyway, I'd been for many years on the positive side, you see, but he turned me over and shoved some jelly in me and he got cracking. I'd never been done like that before, like he did it. Terrific it was. I thought I was going up to the ceiling. He was only a young chap but he'd got a colossal tool. We used to clasp each other very tightly and then when he came he'd just hold me tight. And do you know that he used to come round to my flat nearly every night for months. Mm. So I was well run in! He was a sailor you know, he used to come up from Portsmouth. All the sailors did. And I was really ill after he chucked me up. Yeah, I was, I didn't want to live.

'Over from Pompey for the weekend.'

47

SANDIE: I had an affair with a woman who was very aggressive. She came from central London and she was a daughter of a boxer and he taught her how to box. When she left, she cleared me out, she took every stick of my furniture, left me with an empty flat. An empty flat and a dog which she didn't want to take. Too much trouble and worth nothing. She was like a little boy. Physically attractive and about as immature as I was. She cared a lot about me and, looking back, I would think that, perhaps if we'd been older and wiser, we might have made it, you know. Even though she was, in a lot of ways, very, very tough. But she could also, equally, be very, very sensitive. She wrote beautiful poetry and she had a lovely singing voice. She used to sing to me sometimes and I still miss that. She had a very melodic voice. One of her favourites was 'Scarlet Ribbons'. Sometimes she used to sing me to sleep. It was lovely. I still think about it from time to time.

GILL: The way Sheila and I got together, it was as though it was meant to be. Laurie'd just come out of hospital and she was still in bed, in effect, at home. She was an old friend I'd met on my first visit to Pigott's. So I said, 'Well, I'll go and look after her and live with her till she's better.' She'd got a separate room, so I moved in with her. She didn't seem to get any better. Anyway, one day the surgeon turned up and said she possibly only had three months left to live, so I decided I was going to devote all the time I could to making her last days happy. I started inviting people in to see her and Sheila was one of the ones that I invited. I invited her and Lisa to eat 'cause I found that it was easier to cook for a few people rather than just myself.

I wasn't aware that anything different was happening. I wasn't aware that anything was happening between us at all, until one night. Lisa arrived and Sheila was late. I kept on looking out of the window and I thought, 'What's the matter with me? Why am I so concerned that she's late?' And I couldn't understand myself, my own feelings. It wasn't impatience or anything, I was just totally concerned that she was late. And I looked out at one point and saw her and the whole of my insides sort of leapt with joy at seeing her.

I knew from that moment that I was in love with her. It wasn't sexual at all. I mean, always before it had been a longing to leap into bed with someone, it wasn't with her. It was just I wanted to be with her and that was it. And then, that particular evening, I told Laurie that I loved her. I said, 'I love you and I love Lisa but I'm in love with Sheila.' Later, when Lisa had gone and we were left together and we were talking away, Sheila said, 'Can I kiss you?' and she came over and kissed me. I just burst into tears. It was just wonderful and I'd never had that wonderful feeling before. She does that to me when she kisses me now — but I don't burst into tears now!

AILEEN: I had a most horrible habit. If I saw a hole I couldn't resist putting my finger in that hole and 'Rip!' And there was the most famous scene with Harriet, and she got so angry at it, stormed out of the room, came through with a pair of cords I had just bought and a pair of scissors in her hand. And she was trying to cut through the leg and she couldn't start because the seam was so thick, you see. And eventually she did, she cut the leg off. *Sheer* satisfaction And then she looked at me and I love only (2) you.

It's a feeling im not used to. I've always been so free and easy, it's wonderful to feel you belong to someone. Don't ever leave me Sandie, I know I couldn't do without you now. Would it do anything to you if I said, "I forbid you to ever leave me." I don't look anything like Kirk Douglas but it doesn't stop me using his lines.

I've been thinking what you said about me having a series of crushes. You may be right you know. I don't think I could have felt any deep emotion or jealousy untill I met you. All that passing from day to day trying to find my own understanding is over, ive found you.

The Well of loneliness is more
Than rightly named.
In it are emotions which
can't be caught or Tamed
Once I fell into its gloomy depths
Came out again with lagging
steps.
But I was filled with dark
despair
At what I felt whilst I was
there
I fought hard with my
emotions
To rid myself of my queer
notions
But always do I have that
fight
Io what's wrong instead of do
right
Why do I feel the way I do
This question I can find
no answer to.

Top left Love letter to Sandie, c.1962.
Top right A poem from Sheila's notebook, 1958.
Left A page from Eric's diary, 1967.

27 FRIDAY (27-338)

I met Kenneth A PREEDY just by Palace Pier I went down the steps and so did he and said how mild it was. It was his 22 birthday, and we went on a long journey to the Lonely mans Beach - both of us rather suspicious, he was but more curious. We walked back as far as King Alfred and then on a bus to the Station. We had a drink and he rang up his mother, and I gave him 10/- I think I'll write to him.

28 SATURDAY (28-337)

Sun rises 7.45 Sun sets 4.42   Moon rises 7.41 p.m. Moon sets 9.21 a.m.

Caught 5.25 Brighton Belle and spent a very unhappy night at the Colony Room. I drank a lot of quick whiskies which made me say unsuitable remarks and was told to leave - in fact nobody wanted to talk to me. I may never go to London again at least not for social reasons smiled and she cut the other leg off. I said, 'Just what I wanted, a pair of shorts.'

GEORGE: We used to have spectacular rows. Tell you one we had. In this flat there was a corridor through, with glass doors. And we had a pull-down oven, it was a brand-new pull-down oven, it was about the only brand-new thing we had — that you lit. Well, Steve was in the kitchen, and he was about to light the oven, okay. Well, we had this spectacular row and we left the kitchen, went to the bedroom, ended up in the lounge and I was still hurling abuse at him and he was hurling abuse at me and he thumped me one and rushed off down the passage to the kitchen, slammed the door, I went to say 'Don't!' and I put my fist right through it. At that point he lit the cooker, which he'd left the gas on. There was a godalmighty explosion. The cooker blew. All the top went off. The cooker door shot down with a sheet of flame which went right up the front. The cooker door hit his legs and the sheet of flame went up. The whole front of his hair was singed, and his eyebrows, and he screamed 'I've lost my legs! So I rushed into the kitchen to pull down his trousers and see if he's got any legs and I said 'But you've got legs!' And the thing was, the door had numbed him. And when you think of it, it's ridiculous, I'm pulling his trousers down and the cooker's ablaze and the kitchen's wrecked, with a hole in the glass . . . And the woman upstairs, we had her down at Christmas, she said, 'I hear your little squabbles from time to time.'

GRANT: I knew one couple who had a marriage ceremony. Ooh, my God, how awful! I do remember. They had a very big party and the bride wore white. She suffered with myopia, needless to say she didn't see the husband in the true light. I think it lasted about a year. It was ridiculous, there was a wedding cake, I'd never seen anything so stupid, and a veil, and a bouquet that was flung to a bridesmaid! Well, we were all pissed, of course. I think they got married in a cottage somewhere, probably Black Lion Street.

PETER: The fashionable dress in the early fifties was, definitely in summertime, your grey flannels — jeans weren't in vogue in those days — grey flannels and sports shirt with the sleeves turned up and if you didn't want a tie you wore a cravat and you invariably had to have brown shoes or brown suede shoes. Sometimes gaily coloured stockings — and when I mean 'gaily' I mean just lisle diamond shape black and white — those were the sort of thing. Your stockings could be a little bit outrageous. You'd stand out in the street, you were classed as 'one of those' but it didn't mean much. There was no seriousness in it because they didn't really know, there was a lot of normal people used to wear brown suede shoes and grey flannel trousers and cravat. But that was the fashion, particularly on the Sunday lunchtime.

SANDIE: We had to go to shops where the clothes could be taken back. It meant going in, finding clothes that were liked and that would possibly fit, pretending that they were being bought for a brother, taking them all home and trying them on, and carting them back if they didn't fit, and trying another set. So it really was a performance. But that did mean that you could buy from anywhere because you didn't have to try them on there and make an exhibition of yourself.

GRANT: Brighton queans all wore terribly flared trousers and terribly Hawaiian shirts with all sorts of tulle at the neck. Hairdos were rather flamboyant, it was all out of a bottle. Handkerchiefs, kerchiefs round their neck for scarves. Jewellery, of course, was the greatest thing, they loved jewellery; they used to have not one bracelet but about *four*. And rings on everything except the thumb. Colour-wise it was a bit grotesque. Pink velvet trousers with a green shirt. Rather like Quentin Crisp. Everybody smoked and invariably you could find a queer by the way he held his cigarette.

MARGARET: A lot of them used to dress in very tailored suits. A lot of the women used to have their hair all Eton cropped and Brylcreemed down and they'd wear tailored jackets and skirts and lisle stockings and brogue shoes. And some would wear ties but not a lot of women wore trousers then. I found a pair for twenty-five shillings, a pair of red cords and I lived in them for about three years. But I wasn't allowed to wear them at home so when I went out with Vivienne I used to roll up this pair of trousers and take them with me and change, put them on in the ladies' toilet at the station or somewhere.

BARBARA: You would always have a little finger ring on your left hand, that was another sign. So if somebody was out in the gear, you'd give them the glad eye or they'd give you the glad eye. You always had a little finger ring, whether you were butch or fem. Or you'd wear a wedding ring if you were fixed up with somebody, on your other hand. There you are, third finger right hand, still wearing mine, wouldn't come off now, beautiful wedding ring, worn so thin.

SANDIE: Usually butch girls went to men's hairdressers to get their hair cut, usually the same hairdresser. They would find a hairdresser who accepted them, who understood and then the word would go round and everybody would turn up at the same hairdressers. Certainly in Brighton there was one guy up in Kemp Town who used to cut all the girls' hair. The only disadvantage of that was that they all came out looking the same.

I used to backcomb my hair like mad, my poor hair. I don't know how I survived the experience, but I used to backcomb it frantically at one time, used to take me *hours*. Oh, washing and drying and setting my hair was a total nightmare! It took a half day to do it, and if I was going out — and you always went out on a Saturday evening — I would start all this performance at about two o'clock in the afternoon to get out for about seven or eight o'clock at night. Oh help, it was really dreadful. Fancy having all that.

BARBARA: You'd want to go into this character, so you would dress to feel the part because usually your partner would want you to look like

❝ She dressed to please me. She'd have her hair done every Saturday and we'd go out Saturday night. She'd look great.
VICKY **❞**

51

> **"** I bought a pair of suede chukka boots with a zip up the side and that was queer, that was poof. You wore them, you got your number marked. Pink shirt was definitely queer, colourful clothes were definitely queer. Filk'ns had the daring clothes of the day. I would walk up and down two or three times past that shop just to get glances at these things rather than actually stop and look at them.
>
> GEORGE **"**

you belonged to her, like you were feminine and you belonged to her, and so you would do it almost to please her, besides pleasing yourself. She would say if she didn't like something, she'd say, 'Oh, I think you look awful in that dress, for heaven's sake take it off.' Or you'd buy something new, she'd say, 'Oh, I think you look beautiful in it. Yes! Wear it.'

VICKY: I suppose I always was a bit butch. I was the only one at college to have a drape blazer and a DA haircut. I was a Teddy-girl. I wore suede shoes with crepe soles. I never had a blue suede pair. I think grey was my favourite colour, I had a very pale grey coat with a black velvet collar. And we used to wear a high neck, like a shirt, but not a shirt because women didn't wear shirts then. And there used to be a velvet band that you'd put round your neck with a big cameo brooch in the middle. That was ace, yes, that was top. And my hair was dark then and I used to have a Tony Curtis haircut which was all curly in the front and at the back it was all slicked back in a DA. Anything you see at the pictures of Teddy-girls, then it was exactly what I did.

DENNIS: During the war you didn't wear underclothes because you couldn't get them. I didn't wear any underclothes until I was about eighteen, when I got my first pair of Y-fronts, which I thought were ever so outrageous. I'd seen them advertised in American magazines, because they came over from America. Apart from that, all you had was horrible flannel things that were nasty, anyway, and revolting. And when I got these Y-fronts, I thought they were fabulous.

JAMES: But we must go on to the Filk'ns. Phil and Ken ran a gentlemen's dress shop, a gentlemen's casual wear shop called Filk'n, 'Filk'n Casuals'. Phil and Ken. But they wanted it pronounced like 'Fucking Casuals', again, very daring. It was next to the Theatre Royal stage door in Bond Street. And they were the first people to do beach shirts and shorts in gaudy, jazzy, Caribbean-type colours for gentlemen. Really, in those days, you wouldn't be seen dead in that sort of thing, you'd be thought to be *that* sort of person. But they did very well, and probably at that time were the only people in Britain, I would imagine. I can't think of anything in London quite as camp as that. They would do a few other things in addition to beachwear. They were so outrageous that it was always said that if you went to buy a tie they'd measure your inside leg. Phil was always known as Rose Filk'n, and Ken was known as Esme Filk'n and they really were very, very naughty.

They're both dead now. They were absolutely outrageous, but like so many queans of the time although they made a good business, they weren't exploiting us financially. They were also generous in their private life. They ended up with a two-storey maisonette on the corner of Grand Avenue and Church Road. Two storeys of a huge Victorian or Edwardian mansions. They did this place up beautifully with crystal chandeliers and great velvet curtains in dirty greens and a grand piano with the Spanish shawl on top and all. In the most expert, exquisite taste, very expensive. In fact they came to grief eventually because they'd spent more money than they'd taken, or rather they were spending their takings rather than their profits.

HARRY: Phil and Ken sold casual shirts, jackets, trousers and underbriefs, which were brief underbriefs like they wear them today, which were very daring in those days. They used to make them out of odd materials. They had a whole range of them done in cotton gingham, those red gingham squares and blue gingham squares, and they used to be all tailored, and the pouch was shaped at the front with a seam down it. They did lovely shirts. And Esme did a lot of leather stuff.

It was very daring to wear their sort of clothes, you didn't find it anywhere else. The nearest thing to their underwear were Y-fronts which were quite big, but these were proper briefs with sides. They used to make them in several sizes, they used to make dozens of them. They had this little shop and on a Saturday I used to call in and see them. I'd sit at the back, downstairs in the workroom and there'd be a trail of people coming in. They did very well indeed, and this was before Vince started: they were the first ones to do it, and then gradually other people caught on and the trade dropped off a bit . . . People used to come down specially for a weekend in Brighton and to go round to Aunt Rose's shop. It was busy all day long on a Saturday.

EDDIE: In the sixties, style started to change, people started to wear bright colours. If you wore a yellow sweater, it was considered very, very way out. And it was all happening in Brighton; people were wearing red socks, that was the start of the red socks. And I remember about six of us, we all went into a shop and all bought a purple tie, we were all wearing purple ties. And they used to sell Sobranie cocktail cigarettes, and they were gold! And blue! And we'd go round smoking these. People became aware of colour, they started wearing different colours and started dyeing their hair. Then there was a craze for the Italian style. We used to call them bumfreezers, because the jacket was very short at the back. And winklepicker shoes, greased hair; everybody wore their hair greased, slicked back. It was the Teddy-boy era.

SANDIE: The fashions of the early sixties used to be these enormous skirts with layers and layers of tulle petticoats that we used to spend hours dipping in starch and drying, hanging all around the kitchen and all over the place. Of course, in those days we never had cars, like young people seem to have willy-nilly today, we went everywhere by bus. We used to get on the bus and we used to have to sit on the side seat. You couldn't sit on the seat that faced front because they would crush your skirts, so you looked for a side seat. And when you sat down, the thing practically came up over your head because there was so much of it! And those tight elastic belts, clip belts round your waist, and quite low-fronted jumpers. That was the way I dressed as a fem then.

VICKY: Our first visit to a club, I had a skirt on. I'd never had a pair of trousers on in my life, I'd always worn skirts. I sat there fascinated, the whole night. We were just outsiders, they didn't know us, we weren't dressed like them. Well, I took a good look at what was going on around me. I thought, 'Well, next time I come back, I'll have trousers on.' So during the week I went into a men's shop and bought a pair of trousers. Well, it was

66 As it got on into the sixties, then you'd wear chiffon and things like that, but you wouldn't wear them in the fifties. BUCK 99

53

embarrassing. They wouldn't let me try them on, which I took umbrage at, and I said, 'Why can't I try them on?' and they said, 'Well, they're men's changing rooms only.' I said, 'Well, that's ridiculous!' Nevertheless, I bought the pair, I took a gamble, took them home, and all I had to do was turn them up. I had fights with various shops. And I had the manager down in the men's department of one large clothing store. I said, 'This isn't fair! If I want to buy men's trousers, I should be allowed to buy men's trousers and have the privilege of trying them on, like anybody else in this store. If you're not going to let me into your men's changing rooms because you're frightened I might chase all the men away, then let me take the trousers up to the women's changing rooms.' So after a long argie-bargie, they agreed that wasn't too much to ask for, and I was escorted by somebody from the men's department up to the women's department to go to the changing rooms. The next week I was back at the club in trousers and a men's shirt which I'd bought off the counter from somewhere. And a coat. I felt much more comfortable, much more at ease. Jean wore ordinary women's clothes, which she did through all our life together. Jean was very feminine and has never changed.

GEORGE: I had a very funny incident happen to me. This guy, quite clearly a policeman in plain clothes, came up to me and said could he ask me questions about homosexuality. And I ran, because I wasn't sure whether this guy was either genuinely a policeman trying to investigate — because I'd heard something about how they were going to have some sort of investigation, and I assumed maybe that was part of it — or whether I was being picked up, I'll never know, but I know I fled. And no way, Jose! Off I went ! I must have been pretty obvious for him to come up and do that though, mustn't I? I was in tight black drainpipe trousers which were all the rage then, and brothel-creepers and a cerise-coloured suede jacket. I suppose that was quite bold. Yeah, clothes were quite bold.

JANICE: The mid-sixties was the birth of everybody beginning to change, people didn't wear suits and frocks so much, it was more unisex. And people were coming out with bright colours, as indeed was the rest of the country. I mean, it wasn't exclusive to the gay scene, it was a time of fashion change . . . more independence for the young, generally, I think.

VICKY: By the mid-sixties we still wore trousers and perhaps waistcoats, and frilly shirts were in then, the Tom Jones frilly shirt was in, but I certainly don't think we were wearing ties. Stopped ties, ties went out. But when jeans came in, I got jeans, and I got out of real trouser trousers. I followed fashion.

ANNIE: I always wore trousers, all my life. When I could possibly get out of a skirt, I did. I usually wear men's trousers. They don't fit me, women's trousers, because I don't have any hips. So I've always bought men's trousers. I never wore a tie. I only wore men's clothes because they were so much more comfortable, and so much more workmanlike. Because I was always having to do — and wanting to do — the sort of jobs that men do, like the wiring and the plumbing, and the painting and the gardening,

54

Left Grant at the Sussex Arts
Ball.
Above Grant as a principal
boy at the Sussex Arts Ball.

and all those things. I can do them as well as most men. And so you have to wear men's clothes. And also, it didn't appeal to me, particularly, to dress up and make up and have my hair done and look feminine.

HARRIET: In the clubs, I suppose women did tend to dress in roles, butch and fem, but then I've always worn slacks or trousers all my life, even before slacks were popular. It was very rare, very difficult to get slacks really, but it gives you the freedom of movement. I don't think I wore them because it looked butchy or something, because I don't think I like men enough to want to be like them. It's just you have the freedom of getting over stiles when you're walking, and keeping your money in your pockets and everything; wonderful freedom.

GRANT: In the fifties, one of the big things about Brighton was the Arts Ball and it was held at the Aquarium. And it was really quite something. It was known all over England. In fact we used to say that a certain number of queans used to spend the whole of the summer sitting on the Men's Beach, sewing sequins on the gowns. And they sewed them on by the hundredweight, not by the dozen. The Aquarium was quite a big place and it held about a hundred, I suppose. At first they turned a blind eye to anybody in drag but then it got a little bit hilarious and they wouldn't permit drag for the last two or three years and finally it was shut. But it was really quite hilarious, it was from about nine or ten at night to about two or three in the morning. It was extremely well-run. There was no trouble. They didn't have any bash-ups or people throwing chairs around.

Some of the costumes must have cost hundreds. It was fantastic. I mean, ostrich feathers in those days when the salaries were five pounds a week, some of those ostrich feathers were seven pounds, just one feather, and they probably had twenty on a headgear. Quite a big thing, the Arts Ball.

Collie Knox.

PATRICK: Brighton has always had a gay mafia — all the expensive queans, you know, throwing cocktail parties, with art dealers and old actresses. It was a very closeted place, there was an awful lot that went on behind heavily brocaded curtains. Robin Maugham lived down here and had crowds of the camp coming to visit. Terence Rattigan had a house here. Collie Knox, Dougie Byng, Gilbert Harding, Alan Melville, Sir David Webster . . . And Godfrey Winn lived out at Falmer. And they'd all have these pink champagne and sherry dos — 'Oh, we must invite Enid Bagnold.'

KAY: Sex and money was at the heart of the gay community in Arundel Terrace, Lewes Crescent and Chichester Terrace. It was an upper-class jungle. When I came here it wasn't such a mixed social group as it is now. The Terrace had a class thing about it, moneyed thing.

I would be invited to cocktail parties which isn't my thing. Gay males, rich, living in swanky, elegant — piss-elegant — places, ghastly taste, actually, to my mind, with the interior decorator boyfriend. They considered themselves classy; worked in the Theatre, banking, stockbrokers. They had all these cocktail parties full, also, of what we called the bridge ladies who liked faggots. And theatrical lezzies. Nothing was worse than theatrical lezzies of that period. They were even more superficial than everyone. They quarrelled all the time, they drank too much. They were all refined and ladylike, as it were, and then suddenly you'd realise they'd just had too many gins, so they'd start on each other: snip, snip, snip, snip. Sad. I don't think they liked me, really, because I wouldn't play.

After appearing once or twice, I just went back to, 'I'm an eccentric writer.' It lacked intellect. It was no different from straight cocktail parties to which I was asked by the same kind of nit-wits. It was gossip, always innuendo, gossip, which I can't bear. It was just boring, frankly. And they always had a coffee table full of the latest books, which they never read. I wasn't used to this sort of chi-chi. I can't bear trendiness.

JANINE: I was having lots of affairs with lots of women in the WRAC, and I used to come back to Brighton with various girlfriends. I was mad about driving, partly because of my mother's influence, but I always rallied. I had two Morgans, a Lotus Esprit. I'd had some super cars from the age of eighteen onwards and so I was always the one, even with the gay men, who sort of organised these things. It was a question of piling, four, five, six people in the car and going down. And of course, not wanting to be seen by my parents who knew everybody in Brighton. So we had to come down either very early in the morning after a Saturday night party in London or something like that and we used to rush down to Black Rock because I knew that bit best. I knew all the pools, Black Rock pool and everything and the beaches round there and I used to take all my gay friends down there and we'd have a marvellous sort of day, eating out at the good restaurants in Brighton, and having a good time, but me always absolutely terrified that I was going to bump into not only my parents but friends of my parents, because they were legion.

JOHN: Around that time a lot of my friends were coming down. I had a house at number 4 Castle Street, and a lot of my friends came down wanting to stay for the weekend and odd days in between, and so I decided to turn my house into a guest-house and let them pay, albeit very reasonable. It covered the cost of all the entertaining. So it was eventually called the Chateau Gaye, and it was quite successful but it doesn't take much to fill a small house in Brighton, especially when you get nice weather in the summertime, and people wanting to go to Telscombe Beach and so on . . .

JO: Now I'm trying to think when I started coming to Brighton. I suppose it would have been in the fifties, the early fifties. What were the clubs? There was one called Pigott's, on the corner of Madeira Place and St James's Street, and there was a hotel next door, called the Atlantic. There weren't any gay hotels then, you know, so I'd stay at this Atlantic, which was

Jo and girlfriend.

straight, but we knew it and it was quite clean and wholesome and central. My mum and pop used to come and stay in it as well, and I used to bring whichever bird I happened to be with for a dirty weekend. And then there was the Greyhound, we used to go there, the 42, which although it was mainly boys, if you were an accepted woman and not a sort of diesel dyke looking for punch-ups, they let you in. But the Curtain was very, very nice, that was very mixed.

MARGARET: I decided we'd have to have some transport to get about — we'd have a motorbike. So we went to Pride and Clark, in Brixton, and had a look at the motorbikes, and they had a lot of ex-army bikes in there, so we decided we were going to have one of these. Great big green, army-green bike. It was ninety-nine pounds, and I think we'd saved enough to put two pounds down as a deposit, and the rest was over about three years. And we bought this bike, an enormous thing. It was a rigid frame and it had two seats, one for the pillion and one for the rider. So Pride and Clark showed us how to work the gears and we got this bike back and I passed my test on it — put in for a test straight away and passed it, and decided to paint this bike. So we painted it black. Every Sunday we used to get up about half past seven in the morning and whizz down to Brighton. We always used to go up to St Dunstans. We didn't know about it being a gay place or anything like that, we both just liked Brighton.

JAN: And then someone suggested Brighton. They'd heard that Brighton was a real swinging town so there was five of us that piled into a car, an old Vauxhall Viva, wonderful engine, they were absolutely renowned for being rust-buckets. And we drove down on a Saturday, it took what? . . . about three hours, something like that. And we went to this club, I can't remember the name, I know it was Bedford Square and that was great, and that was when I realised that there were such things as butch and fem, because in Clacton we all just used to wear trousers and sort of sloppy sweatshirts. These women really looked like men, you know. I could never actually understand it. And these very, very feminine women were just something I could never understand but it was fun, it was good. I didn't realise there were so many about.

We all sort of kipped in the car, slept just enough. We used to drive back on the Sunday. It was fun, it was just a big hoot really, but as I say, it was the dress that I couldn't get over. I mean there were a few in Clacton that used to wear ties and suits but nothing quite so outrageous as there was down in Brighton. It was just a completely different world, totally different.

VERA: Came down to Brighton nearly every weekend. Oh yeah, with Joy and her little girl and the little car, it was an old banger then. We lived in Earls Court, and it was easy to go up through Putney, over Putney Bridge, on to the Kingston bypass, up past Dorking on the Brighton Road. We didn't go to the clubs or anything because she had the little girl. We just used to go down to the funfair, take the kid on the games and things like that. Joy loved cockles and whelks and ice-cream, and I said, 'How can you eat all that?' We used to go in a pub and have a drink and just have a normal weekend in Brighton, sort of thing, there was nothing gay in it at all.

SIOBHAN: I've always had a bike of some sort, Honda 50s, 70s and 90s, and I spent hours coming down on those bikes so I knew the A23 as it was with all its little winding bits off by heart and I loved it. I loved the journey down, I spent hours coming down here, and hours going back. I was always coming down here.

VICKY: Every now and again the people who ran the Robin Hood in London would have a coach party and they'd take us, the favourite place of course was Brighton because that was the gay Mecca, and we'd do a tour of all the clubs, get absolutely paralytic. They'd pick you up at a certain point in London, in this coach with crates of God knows what went on. All women. You'd come down to Brighton and they'd take you down to where the Aquarium is, that's where the coach would disgorge us all and from there on we'd go through the town. We'd arrive in the daytime, we'd go for lunch somewhere, and then we'd go and find everything. I mean, I didn't know anywhere at the time so really we sort of trailed along behind people who did. And we ended up in some weird and wonderful places, little clubs over the top of shops and all kinds of things that I've never been able to find since I've been here so they must have been long gone.

SIOBHAN: Brighton was known to be a bit . . . you were supposed to come and have a good time down here, you didn't come down for quiet walks on the seafront in the mist, you came to have a laugh and to get drunk and to go to these little clubs and to vomit up your breakfast the next morning. We all loved it, we used to spend lots of money doing it as well.

JANICE: Those outings were a special treat, really. What we used to do was get a crowd of people from Gateways. We used to get about four car loads of us with about ten people crammed into each car, scream down what was then the A23 and we'd go off, usually to the Variety Club, that closed down at some point, so we ended up going to the Queen of Clubs, which was at the top of the square. Very seedy little hole, oh, indeed it was. We used to get a lot of hookers go there, I remember, when the pubs shut because I think in the winter the pubs used to close about half past ten. The club didn't close until twelve and even then it used to stay on, we'd stay there until about two o'clock or something, nobody seemed to worry. It was decidedly seedy, very small.

JO: I remember once, we were living in Golder's Green at the time and my mum said she'd run out of bread, it was on a Sunday. And I said, 'Come on, it's a nice day, we'll go and get a loaf,' and I don't know how it happened, we finished up on the South Circular and we finished up at the Curtain Club in Brighton. And my mum played on the machine and she won the jackpot and she thought she had to spend all her money in the club. And nobody enlightened her, we just let her and she bought us all drinks.

VERA: Margaret and I used to come down to Brighton, used to come to Brighton often, come early in the morning, bring a picnic, Margaret used to make a picnic, we used to sit up on the Downs. But we never went to the clubs, Margaret and I never went to the clubs, we used to go and have

"
Everyone used to go down to Brighton quite regularly. You could go on the morning paper train for 1/6d return, and you'd get there about seven. And nearly all the hotels, men could walk in and get a double bed. It was generally recognised, if you wanted to have a good day, you went to Brighton — as long as you knew where to go.
ARTHUR "

a drink or bring a picnic and sit on the front, or we used to go on the hills past St Dunstans and up on the green there, that was mostly where we went because I enjoyed being up on the hill and watching the cliffs and all that. We walked all along there, by Roedean. We used to say, 'Nancy Spain went to Roedean.' You felt a connection, you see, because you knew she was gay.

MARGARET: We used to come to Brighton, this was one of the things that Kenric used to do at the weekends, the whole group. We used to go on treasure hunts and at the weekends we used to come down to Brighton. We said, 'Well, we're going down to Brighton and we're going to camp out for the weekend. Anybody want to come?' And all these various other people said, 'Yes! Yes!' And we would all come down here and we'd all bring our tents and all the people who hadn't got tents would sleep in their cars. We found a good parking spot for camping on the road from the top of Dyke Road Avenue, Hove Golf Course is up there, and there was a big space of green between the road and the golf course. And we pulled off and we used to pitch our tents up there. And that was great. Somebody must have known about a club in Middle Street called the Variety Club, so we used to spend the day — we'd come down on the Saturday, go to St Dunstans, sit out on the grass and eat our picnics and sunbathe. I suppose we had a wash somewhere, perhaps we had a wash and a brush-up at the pier, I don't know, but we found out about this Variety Club and we got ourselves in there. There's now a school in Middle Street. And they had a room downstairs with a roulette wheel, and I liked a bit of a gamble, so we went in there, and we would have a drink — a whole crowd of us, about fifteen — and we'd play the roulette game and when we'd had enough we'd go back to our tents and we'd light a fire and we'd go round the golf course, and any wooden posts we'd pull them all up, we put them all on the fire, and we'd sit round this fire — it's a wonder the police never came round — and we'd have a sing-song. And then we'd douse the fire and get in our tents . . .

And then in the morning we'd all be up early and we must have taken canisters of water because we used to wash and clean our teeth and everything up there. And then we'd come down to the West Pier and there's — it's still there today — there's a little restaurant opposite the West Pier, an Italian place, Toni's, and we'd all go in to Toni's and have our breakfast and then various people would do various things. We seemed to spend our time going up and down the West Pier.

DENNIS: I had a week's holiday and I thought, 'Where shall I go?' And then I remembered one of the guys I met doing National Service, Bobby, had been down to Brighton and had a fabulous time, so I wrote to him and said, 'Where did you stay?' and he wrote back and said he stayed with a guy called Richard Stone who had a guest-house in Lansdowne Place, 105. So I wrote to Richard Stone and came down for a week. That was in July of 1955 or it might have been August. I went to this bar, it was the back of Sherry's ballroom. And there was this fabulous blond barman, called Phil, and I looked at him and I thought, 'Oh!' and I sat on a bar-stool and I spent the whole week, I didn't see very much of Brighton that week, I must admit, I spent most of the time, certainly within opening hours, sitting on that stool gazing at Phil and going, 'Ohhhhhh.'

Top left Day trip from the
Robin Hood Club in London.
Left Vera at work as a
forecourt attendant, late fifties.
Top right Vera with her car.
Above Vera and Jo.

61

VICKY: We had a wonderful holiday. We stayed in a bed and breakfast place in Hove which was very smart. I don't think they knew what had hit them when we arrived. Oh God! It was absolutely dead straight and we arrived there, dear, all hell let loose and there were silences when we went into breakfast. Still, we had a really good holiday. Absolutely two weeks of . . .

William Teeling, MP for Brighton Pavilion, 1944-1969.

GRANT: But then, things were different then, they used to come for a fortnight's holiday. I can remember lots and lots of friends phoning me up or writing to me and saying, 'Ooh, we're coming to Brighton for our usual holiday, we're staying at so-and-so, can we meet you?' Well, they don't come to Brighton now for their holiday. They just don't come. And that stopped at the end of the sixties, beginning of the seventies. They started going abroad. Holland, Morrocco, Spain.

JANICE: Quite often we would go down for the day, on a Saturday say, and spend some time on the beach and then go to the 42 Club at lunchtime 'cause it was open at lunchtime; spend some time, that was nice, I liked that. It was actually a boys' bar, I think, but you used to get some quite famous people in there. You'd get a lot of Members of Parliament, whoever they were at the time, go in there and a lot of the pop scene used to pop in there, have a drink, male and female, and it was nice, had a piano in there — I remember one of the old boys used to play it occasionally.

♥   ♥   ♥

RICHARD: In Brighton, going to clubs, which I'd never been to before, was my real introduction into a gay world. I was absolutely terrified, didn't feel I belonged in it, because it was so against everything that I'd ever known. I don't mean morally speaking, it was just that it was drinking — which was something that my father was very much against — and staying up half the night and all this sort of thing, which I wasn't used to. Also it was a culture-shock: when you walk into a bar, and there's men dancing and kissing and cuddling one another, and screaming, 'Darling!' across the floor; I mean, it is a real shock to somebody that's never seen it before.

❝ I'd never been used to the queer clubs before I came to Brighton. Frightened me to death! Terrified me. I thought it was something I shouldn't be doing by entering the door. I thought I was breaking the law. Frightened me to death it did. PETER ❞

SHEILA: I started going to Pigott's in 1950 when I was twenty and it was mostly girls but there were one or two men there, some of the boys were there. Dolly played the piano. This little lady used to play at the piano with her jangling bracelets; cigarette hanging on her mouth. And we used to have this sing-song, the old tunes, 'Don't laugh at me cos I'm a fool' that's right, 'Freight Train', that was Laurie's tune. Oh yes, they used to stand up at the piano. It's not a very big pub. I think the bar went in a sort of a half moon and there was only one entrance. It was terribly small, there was room enough for a piano, and there weren't many seats. It was quite tatty, all really dark brown. It was just ordinary working-class. There weren't any professionals there, they probably had their own places to go.

GILL: I was travelling down and they'd told me that Pigott's was the place to go but I couldn't find Pigott's 'cause I didn't know Brighton. Eventually I found it and walked in. I was quite disappointed actually, it was like somebody's front room. I was quite early there, I was probably the first one in and two people floated in and then the girls started arriving and I think Laurie and Dot arrived. I was terrified, because I'd heard all these tales, I'd heard it from the boys' side, the boys had to be careful when they went in these pubs because they were groped and they daren't go to the toilets else they'd get raped. And I'd put it round to the women's side, you see. They'd told me about these very butch females and, 'Are you butch or fem?' And I thought, 'What on earth are they talking about?' So I was very apprehensive when I came down here and the amount of beer, Double Diamond, that I used to drink, I think I was absolutely bursting to go to the toilet and I wouldn't go because I was frightened to go down there!

SHEILA: I think normal people used to go to Pigott's for sightseeing. It was noted that it was a gay pub, because in those days people knew exactly where the pubs were because there weren't that many. You'd get ordinary people, fellas or couples come in. They'd probably be out drinking and come in just for a laugh. You'd probably get a few comments but if they were outnumbered, you wouldn't be too bad. They would probably just sit there. The men might make a few remarks, you know, 'Come over 'ere darlin'. What you need is a good man.' Most of our concern was the fact that you'd be there in your regalia — because when you went out you dressed up in your regalia — that you'd be discovered by someone and that would be it, you'd be branded. My biggest fear was that one of my customers would come into the pub. I think I would have died.

GRANT: The Regina Club was the first really lovely club, it became very famous. Well, up until the Regina, all of us in Brighton used to go up Saturday or Sunday and go to the gay clubs in London. And then suddenly a lesbian friend decided that it would be rather a good idea to have one of those rather lavish clubs in Brighton and she got in touch with a man who had a club on Brunswick Terrace, and he moved down to this place over a shop on North Street.

Anyway a friend took me up to this club in North Street called the Regina. And when I went in I was extremely impressed because it had a very grand entrance up a magnificent flight of stairs. The proverbial flight of stairs you see in pantomimes, with Dames coming down. And when we got there I must admit it was breathtaking. It was a beautiful carpet, the whole length of the room was a bar, completely mirrored at the back, with the most beautiful crystal chandeliers you've ever seen in your life. A very nice grand piano in the window. Seats all round the wall, it was so unusual, all the seats were black velvet. The bar was white plastic on top, but cushioned black velvet, the front of it. Everything else was gold, so the whole thing was black and gold. It just hit you as being black and gold. It was very ornate. Anyway we went in, and the owner made us very welcome, he'd got some canned music on. My friend said, 'You've got a nice big piano, haven't you got a pianist? My friend here plays the piano, he'll play for you.' And that's how it started. The music had to be cover for conversation. It wasn't to be

> **I can't remember any black faces around Brighton, really. It would stick in my memory, I'm sure. One only. I can remember one black student, who actually had a bedsit above the Variety Club, who was a lovely lad.**
> JAMES

Pigott's
(The St James's Hotel)

listened to. Although if someone wanted to convey something to someone else without going up and saying it, they would ask me to play whatever it was. There were lots and lots that had meanings to them. 'Can't Help Lovin' Dat Man of Mine', from 'Showboat'. 'I'm in Love for the Very First Time'. 'I'm in Love with a Wonderful Guy'. 'I Feel Pretty', from 'West Side Story'. 'The Party's Over', from 'The Bells are Ringing', I've done that three times. Actually it's a very nice number. 'Hold Me, Thrill Me' was a great favourite with the lesbians. So was 'I Hate Men', from 'Kiss Me Kate'.

Well, it was quite flagrant in the end. He used to be open till two and three in the morning on Bank Holidays and on Saturdays. He got warned — the publicans didn't like him, the publicans went to the police and said, 'It's not right that he's serving booze till two or three in the morning, getting away with it, he must be shut.' And of course, eventually, he got what we used to know as being done. The police walked in one night and the chief inspector of Brighton came with about four detectives, and as soon as they walked in: 'Nobody is to touch what they are drinking. Put your hand over your glass and keep it there.' That was what they shouted through the megaphone. The piano was simply covered with glasses. And then they came round to everyone in the club, 'Name? Address? Do you know that you are drinking intoxicating liquor after time and do you know that this is an offence under the law so and so and so and so? Yes? Right then, you'll hear from us.' Everyone was fined. And of course he shut it, it never re-opened as a club. Then other gay clubs started up — St Albans — another in Montpelier Road, that didn't last.

GERALD: There was a police purge, as far as I can recall, that followed the Police Trials here in 1958. It was alleged that the police were running a protection racket and I think it was proved quite conclusively that there was bribery and corruption going on, on a pretty big scale. An enormous amount of illegal drinking had been going on, in all sorts of bars. The chief constable, Charles Ridge, Detective-Inspector John Hammersley, and Detective-Sergeant Trevor Heath were charged. Now, Ridge was found not guilty; Hammersley and Heath were found guilty, and sentenced. There was the most notorious bar at the bottom of West Street, totally heterosexual, and this late drinking went on with rather rough types, villains, and the racing crowd, and the club was referred to throughout Brighton as the Bucket of Blood, because of the enormous amount of fights that went on down there. And then, of course, the new chief constable that came in jumped on all this illegal drinking, and he also was very much against any gay establishment, no doubt about that. He was very, very anti-gay.

And then everything went into reverse, and a lot of gay places were closed. Indeed, the bar underneath the Royal Albion, that was closed. One Sunday lunchtime, various assistant managers came down and handed cards out to people, saying, 'Your patronage is no longer required. Please drink up and leave.'

GRANT: The police were very naughty. Well, first of all, they didn't like drinking clubs. And they didn't like gay clubs. They had a procedure. First of all it was fire precautions, they'd walk in and say, 'Your fire precautions are not sufficient, get it altered.' Second thing is, they'd come

Contemporary advertisement.

in and they'd say, 'We understand you've been serving drink to people either under age or people that are undesirable. Now watch it, if we catch them again, you're done.' Well, the third thing, they'd just walk in and say, 'You're drinking after time. That's it.' And they'd shut it. They were a bit naughty.

SHEILA: The few times I was taken to the 42 Club, which was men only, I was one of the few women who were there and the boys weren't terribly happy about the situation. They preferred to have a club of their own. But at least with the Variety Club it wasn't too bad. You would mix in pretty well with the chaps.

HARRY: We'd always start the evening in the 42 Club. It was more like a party than a club in there. Everyone would circulate, chatting, chatting, chatting, hearing all the gossip. It was roaring in the 42 Club. There wasn't any television in those days. We had to make our own entertainment.

GRANT: I can remember one Saturday night coming out of the 42 Club and it was quite late because they'd had an extension, and one great big, very tough butch lesbian and her better half who was a very lady-like little thing, we were walking along — there used to be in those days a taxi-rank at the bottom of West Street — and we were walking round there to get the taxi. Of course, it was near Chatfield's and some very leery sailors came out and sent me up very considerably, and this big toughy lesbian went over to the sailor. She said 'What did you say?' He said, 'Yeurgh . . .' you know, very drunk. She was very tall and very tough. He was quite short. She picked him up off the ground and said 'If I get another peep from you, I'll put you straight through that window. Now fuck off!' He ran. She picked him up, just like that, and held him in the air! They were, they were tough, they were big girls. You didn't cross them.

Chatfield's, in the front on West Street, was so raucous and so loud and to some people's taste so disgusting, they would walk down and say, 'How horrible!' Other people would say, 'Let's go in and look at it, let's see.' Everybody was smoking, you couldn't see across the place for smoke. It was *low*, but it was quite fun. It always got very crowded. There were two bars, one was Dennis's bar, Dennis ran it, he was gay and everybody knew Dennis. The other bar was mainly the entertainment side. You got a mixture of people, I mean it was a very rough bar, there was a criminal element, you got crooks in there, not very nice people but the police never closed it down because, if they wanted to look for somebody, they would always go into Chatfield's.

A lot of the clientele were sailors, but of course in sailors uniform, so they were quite easy to spot, and invariably, if they came over from Pompey for the weekend, they had no accommodation. So the great thing was, anybody who had a flat or a house with a floorspace, would probably go down to Chatfield's and chat up a sailor and take him home for the weekend. The sailor was satisfied! The Brightonian was satisfied! And everybody enjoyed it.

> 66 It was quite a den of iniquity in Chatfield's, you'd get all the wide boys and the prostitutes. I didn't frequent nasty places like that. SHEILA 99

JAMES: Someone said to me, 'Whatever you do, don't ever go in the Golden Fleece. It's full of that sort of people.' So the next night I went down there. It was the most notorious of the bars, was the Golden Fleece in Market Street. There were two bars there, one was fairly discreet, presided over by Bert. Bert was an elderly gentleman of a charming character, the soul of discretion, who would listen to all sorts of people's confessions and keep everything well under his hat. The other side was hilarious and riotous, presided over by a gentleman called Dennis whose second name I never discovered. Dennis was one of those flamboyant queans who couldn't give a shit about anybody and had frequently been in trouble for all sorts but always bounced back, larger than life. One of those few, in those days, who would actually probably be too indiscreet and compromise you in public, so not everybody took kindly to him. We had to earn a living in the town, so we didn't really want to be screamed at in the street.

EDDIE: There used to be a great big fat blonde called Queenie, who sat at the bar in the Belvedere, and she was as tough as teak. She was. I've seen her sort out three matelots. Some say she was a lesbian or she was AC/DC. But in those days, you got about five or six different girls in there, gay girls, and you might get an invitation to play cards, they loved playing cards, all night sessions, for money. And you got one or two professional ladies in as well.

GRANT: The Fortune of War and the Belvedere were mostly used by the very big butch lesbians that really looked like navvies, with bovver boots, and suits, and chains. Some, I admit, were quite good company singly but not in a bunch. *En masse*, they were dreadful.

The Quadrant is one of the very old pubs in Brighton. It was moderately quiet in the downstairs bar but upstairs it was a riot, literally a riot, especially on a Saturday. The police used to come, not in one car but in three or four cars, and take them all away. And a lot of them, very often the cause of the trouble, were matelots who had been drinking since lunchtime, probably hadn't bothered about much to eat and had started drinking again at seven and by half past ten they were literally legless. It was extremely difficult to get to the upstairs bar, you went along Air Street and up through a little doorway and up a terrible winding staircase, and when they were drunk, they didn't bother to help them out, they used to get them to the top of the stairs and say, 'Down you go!' And just give them a push.

Charlie Neate used to play the piano in the upstairs bar on a Saturday night in the fifties and early sixties. He was quite clever in remembering all the bawdy, saucy songs, which sometimes he would alter the words of and put his own words according to the situation. The owner was a woman who was an absolute spitting image of Sophie Tucker. Her name was Fay. She would be sitting on a stool at the bar in a black beaded long dress right down to the floor, with a very long cigarette holder, and she would enjoy the fun just as much as the others and join in. But, if a matelot went too far, she was not averse to just pitching him down the stairs and the stairs, as I've said, were very, very dangerous ones. They're still there to this day.

Fortune of War.

Above Ted (top) and Peter, 1968.
Left David

Above Vicky at St Dunstan's.
Right Day-tripping.

68

JAMES: In my day, the Greyhound was the one and it was the upstairs bar only, which was approached by a side door in a side street, and people would be terribly furtive and look both ways or walk past it and then walk back before diving in, for fear of being recognised. In fact it was often known to people, not as the Greyhound, but as the 'G'. And people would phone up and say, 'Are you going out for a drink tonight? Well, I'll see you at the 'G' at eight o'clock.' It was a nice comfortable bar, and it was presided over by two extraordinary ladies who were allowed to run it on behalf of the manager, who pretended he didn't know what sort of bar it was. And they were called Edie and May.

Edie was at the bar and May was at the piano. I suppose from the American jargon they would be known as fag-hags, which always seemed a most unkind and cruel statement because there were a number of elderly and middle-aged ladies who would go to gay bars simply because they knew they could drink and chat with men, without being compromised. Particularly, of course, in those days, single ladies were not quite respectable if they tried to drink on their own and they were held to be fair game for any Lothario who wanted to chat them up and carry them off and so they felt doubly safe in going into gay bars. And they were certainly far from hags, even the older ones were not witch-like creatures preying upon young gay men. On the contrary, they were really quite wonderful characters. Edie, we'd always assumed, had been a divorcee or something. She had that slight touch of scandal which divorcees had in those days but she was terribly kind and used to take little messages, very discreetly, from boyfriends leaving notes for each other and things like that. Even little written notes would be tucked behind the bottles of Babycham on the top shelf and she would never give away the game, she was the soul of discretion. So that was the Greyhound and that lasted for years and years and years.

GEORGE: Between coming out of the forces at twenty and say, twenty-two, there was a sort of in between period, where I wouldn't accept the fact that I was gay. I was very young and very apprehensive about actually going into a gay bar. We thought how daring this would be. So one night, in the summer, we decided we would go into this gay bar, the Greyhound, opposite the cinema along East Street. We got to the Palace Pier and we walked on and we hadn't got the courage to go in. We got practically to Rottingdean, we still hadn't got the courage. But on the way back, we said, '*We* are going *in!*' So we came back along the seafront, back to Pool Valley, we came up through that side street and we pushed open the door quickly and Steve and I fell in the door and to our horror, we found we were in the heterosexual bar and the gay bar was upstairs. So I lowered my voice and went, 'Brown ale, please.' Suddenly out of the corner of our eye, we saw all these people trooping upstairs and I can't tell you how much courage it took to walk from that bar, to go up those stairs because what you were actually doing, in front of all those people was saying, '*I'm* one of *them.*'

And we went upstairs and, of course, when you went up there, being new to it, although you felt more at home, you felt ill at ease because you didn't know the mores, what was going on there, how you did it. Did you just sit down and talk to anybody? Or did you ignore everybody? How did you meet

❝They were all Princesses in the Greyhound. GRANT ❞

The Greyhound.

The Argyle.

other gays? I mean you found them in twos and threes. How did you break into that? We didn't, we just sat there that night, enjoying it.

JAMES: One of the classiest bars was the Argyle Hotel in Middle Street. That was a very, very select hotel, very expensive but very small. Presided over by two ladies, two sisters, the Misses Brown or, as everybody used to say, the Miss Browns, in those days. We're quite sure they didn't really know what was going on but it was a very smart cocktail bar. The only beer, for example, that was sold was a Baby Tolly, which was like a quarter pint of light ale, which was served in something similar to a port glass and that was half a crown! And half a crown for a Baby Tolly was a lot of money. It did keep the roughs out, and it gave a false air of class to the bar.

Two barmen who were there, very, very smart in their dark red jackets, Tony and Michael, and they were always called the Duke and Duchess of Argyle. Michael was deaf and had the most wonderful way of getting the wrong end of the stick.

Those were marvellous days. There was always a real pianist, an Oriental boy who'd played in swish hotel bars in Singapore, and he was there for some years playing songs from shows, which suited the clientele very well indeed. And I can always remember a very shy young man with thick, black hair brushed back, who used to stand at the far end of the bar, a customer, who wouldn't talk to anybody, and I can remember Tony and Michael saying, 'One day that man is going to be a star because he is the most fabulous drag performer and a total extrovert once he gets into a frock, but terribly shy out of it.' And that was Danny La Rue, who would stay there.

SHEILA: I think everybody gradually disappeared from Pigott's. Other clubs had opened up. There was one other pub in Middle Street, the Spotted Dog, that had one bar at the back where the crowd used to go. The front of the bar was normal. Dolly went there. They followed Dolly a lot, the females. She liked the gay crowd so she always played the piano. She had a great following.

JAMES: The Spotted Dog was presided over by a widow, Flo Taylor from the north of England. Again, she knew the score, it was a beer house only, that meant no wines and spirits. And so if you had something from under the counter, you could have a whisky in a half pint beer glass which would be topped up with dry ginger or something, out of sight. But technically speaking, it was a beer house only. But it was fun. It was a very rough, working-class pub but quite popular and there was a marvellous character called Dolly who would go in and play the piano. Gay bars always had pianists who were characters, and Dolly was a tiny little bird of a lady with a grown up-daughter and a friend who was a lady bus conductress and Dolly would play from music only and this dog-eared music would sit on the piano being played. And Dolly wore dozens of large, noisy bangles on each arm so it was like having percussion and bells as well as having piano. And as she played, she would get faster and faster and faster and the turning of the pages, the never ending rustling of these tatty pages, coupled with the ever increasing speed of music and the jangling of the bracelets made her a bit of a character. And she knew a number of rather daring songs of the Music Hall era, like, 'I want a boy': 'I want a boy, Not for a toy, But to enjoy.'

RICHARD: That was really gay, the Spotted Dog then. You very seldom got any heterosexuals in there, they were mainly all gay in there and you never got any women in there, either, it was a place a woman wouldn't go, unless she didn't know and sometimes that happened, a woman would walk in and she'd realise, you know! It was very, very much gay dominated and they'd have one drink and go and be so embarrassed.

GRANT: A lot of queers would say, 'Oh, I wouldn't go into that place, it's frightfully rough and tumble. Oh, they're awfully common in there.' A lot of people wouldn't go to the Spotted Dog, they would go to the Argyle, or perhaps to the Greyhound. There were some other pubs too that was a different level. There were some queer people, queer fellows in there but they were rougher. They kept agreeably apart. I mean, Harrison's Bar on the front, where at one time I played the piano, there were a lot of queer blokes coming from Birmingham, from Walsall, from Newcastle. But we went in during the week, we didn't go in at weekends. That's the only way I can put it.

I suppose it was the 'Queer Set' I mixed in. We were inclined to be a bit snobbish. Because there were queers among the upper, the middle and the lower classes but in those days I think a lot of queers were inclined to be a bit snobbish, they mixed with their own set. They didn't quite appreciate being sent up by perhaps a queer who would be calling out in the road or would whistle after them. A lot of queers would quickly turn their nose up. They had their clientele, their circle. They didn't exactly mix too well. There was a rather unpleasant expression that we used much more than we do now, 'Oh, he's so frightfully common.' You don't hear that now. 'My dear, he's very common.'

DENNIS: I remember coming down from Bradford and apart from the Spotted Dog and Terry's Bar, the Greyhound was gay; little bar at the Greyhound, presided over by a succession of old queans but that was a bit of an elephants' graveyard really. And the 42 Club was the only gay club in the fifties. On the seafront. In its heyday, in the fifties, the 42 Club was packed 'cause it was the only gay club, really. And then Ray opened another one up Middle Street called the Variety Club, which is where the school is now. And so there were two gay clubs. And then a whole profusion of gay clubs just sprang up, all small ones. There was the Regency Club in Regency Square, there was the Queen of Clubs, which Ray opened in Bedford Square, and then, of course, there was the Curtain Club. A guy called Eddie Duff opened that; big, fat, South African man with an Italian boyfriend called Tina. It was all rather nice but rather sedate. It was open in the afternoons and there was a grand piano tinkling away. I mean, it was just really a bar and there was a bit round the back that had a dancefloor but I never saw anybody round there at all, ever. People just congregated round the bar and simply drank and listened to the pianist and it was all rather nice, rather genteel. Everybody there was homosexual but you couldn't call it gay. It was just a mutual meeting place and most of them,

> **"The bars and the clubs were hard to get into, you couldn't just wander into them, you had to know about them, particularly the clubs. Even the bars were a bit off the beat, they were not obvious places. The whole thing was much more underground than now.**
> MICHAEL **"**

the 42 Club, the upstairs bar at the Greyhound, the Spotted Dog, you got all age groups there; they weren't all old but at the same time, everybody sort of behaved themselves and kept a low profile and it wasn't outrageous. It started to liven up towards the end of the sixties, when everything else started to loosen up, when things had got gay and we had got flower power. Well, of course, they had it down here with a vengeance as you can imagine they would. And Ray Bishop took the Heart and Hand in Ship Street and that became very gay indeed, a sort of Aquarium of its day. And then he took the Curtain Club and made that very gay and there was a disco put in with disco lights and the whole place started to swing.

Outside the Variety Club.

JANICE: Although people had said that Brighton was the gay centre of the south, I didn't know where to go. A girl I worked with used to tell me how her sister was gay. She was frightened to invite me back there for tea because of this lesbian sister. And I tell you what, my little heart was going, 'Boom, boom, boom.' I wouldn't have cared if she looked like the back of a bus, I thought, 'We've gotta get round there, gotta get round there for tea.' Anyway, I didn't pay much attention to this sister or tried not to show much attention. I mean, she was a very pleasant girl, as it happens. She went to the Variety Club in Brighton but I didn't know that's what it was called or where it was. And I remember doing my cloak and dagger stuff here. I had a little car by this time, a little Morris, and the girl lived in Worthing. My friend said, 'Oh, she goes every Saturday night to this club.' So, come Saturday night, the following Saturday night, I actually drove round to her house and parked outside and waited for this girl and followed her. Would you believe this, I actually followed her to the Variety Club but I lost her, I lost her when she went up this little side road 'cause I couldn't get up there in the car, so I was foiled yet again. But at least I felt I was a step nearer.

SANDIE: There was a wonderful club that got pulled down and there's a school there now. The Variety Club in Middle Street. And it was on three or four different floors, perhaps three. In the basement, there was a disco. Ohh, that was wonderful. It was the first disco we'd ever been to, gay disco. Yeah, it was terrific, we really used to love it and there didn't seem to be any aggro, any bitching or backbiting and I think that a lot of that was due to the fact that it was a mixed lot, boys and girls together and I liked that, preferred it.

JANICE: The Variety Club was quite a big place, as I remember. And I think the first thing that struck me was the type of women that were there. There were two definite types of gender. There was the sort of shirts and ties brigade, with very cropped hair, and there was the frilly frock brigade. And I found this very hard to hack because I didn't fit into either. I was me and that was that, really. But that was the first gay club I ever went to. The first time also, I think, seeing two girls dance together in the way that they were. I have to say it shocked me. I know I drank a lot to cope with it. I met two friends of Stella's and I thought they were men but they weren't. Actually, it must have looked very strange because Stella was very female and so was I, so that must have looked very odd. In fact, I think it was remarked upon. Well, I loved it. I mean, they were very friendly, very,

very friendly, very kind. We were quite popular that night, I remember. New faces, probably, that usually works and being so female, because I think female lesbians were in short supply. I was, nevertheless, with Stella that night — but I remember thinking it would have been nice if I wasn't!

SANDIE: Oh, the Lorelei coffee bar, yes, we used to half live in there, yes, loved it. In the very beginning, they used to open on a Saturday night, night, after the clubs had closed, and that was super because once the club had closed, we all would go round camping through the streets at all hours of the night and early morning, you know, singing loud songs, one thing and another. We used to behave outrageously, really, when I think about it. But yeah, we used to land up in the Lorelei and it would be crammed to the doors, you know, just drinking coffee. I'm sure people these days just wouldn't bother, if it's non-alcoholic, but we did then and we loved it and it was great fun. And that was a great mix, Lorelei, of boys and girls. It was sad when that went although the two fellas who owned it, they owned it for a long time afterwards, they just stopped doing the Saturday nights. But you'd always see gay people in there and whenever I went to Brighton, I'd always go in there and I'd always see someone gay. But they've been gone a long time now.

VICKY: There was a definite difference between butches and fems, there was a line, a distinct line and you knew where you were. If you were in a club and another butch came up to ask your girl to dance, they never, ever asked the girl, they asked you and if you said it was alright then they asked the girl and the girl could then say no but you were the first and if they didn't ask you, oh, they were in trouble. You wouldn't dare do it, you just wouldn't do it. Well, people used to get smacked around because of it. It was an absolutely immediate response. I mean, it didn't happen to anyone who looked as if they could take care of themselves but if the butch had gone out to the toilet, say, and she came back and found someone talking to her girl then there would be trouble and yes, some would say, 'I'll take you outside.'

SHEILA: Some of the butches were, I suppose, to my mind, even more outrageous than I was. I mean they would blatantly go out, probably in the daytime, dressed up and sit down with their pint of beer. Where I would keep that just for the nights. I never particularly wanted to do that sort of thing. I just wanted to find someone and set up home and settle down and that was all I wanted. I never wanted to be part of any particular scene. I never enjoyed going, really, to the bars and the clubs. I felt a lot of it was a little bit false: all this chopping and changing of partners.

GRANT: The St Albans Club was very nice. They didn't have the same clientele as the Regina Club quite, it was nearer Hove, it was more of the, let's say, 'landed gentry'. Three very fat, very salubrious, very affluent judges used to go to the St Albans, with their boyfriends. Chauffeur used to drive them up in the Rolls, or Daimler, and dump them, and then call for them about three or four hours later. It was that type of club. Very nicely appointed, very nice, very swish. Drinks were a little pricey. I think they did food as well because, if you had a supper licence, you could open to half

66 You tended to be a little discreet when you were going into a club, look up and down the road and make sure that nobody you were working with was around or something like that. Nip out of the car and nip straight down, that sort of thing. But once you were inside you were alright. . .
VALERIE 99

73

eleven. Closing time in those days was half past ten. So of course, they all got supper licences. And, if you'd seen what the suppers were, you would really have laughed your head off. It was probably one mouldy sandwich which was turning up at the edges all round, that had been under a plastic lid for about four days. And no one ever ate it, of course. You had to keep it in front of you on a plate. Quite ridiculous.

JAMES: The St Albans Hotel in Regency Square was run by a couple, Peter Orpin and Ted Irving. Peter was from quite a wealthy Brighton family and Ted was a merchant seaman. They'd palled up years ago and ran this very smart gay hotel. It was a very discreet place, where couples could stay without fear of being suspected or molested. The hotel bar was turned into a members' bar. Despite the propriety and respectability of it, a couple of gentlemen might dance a rather discreet foxtrot together. I remember a marvellous character called Ronnie Boyce, a tall, slim quean with a lisp. He was known as Buttercup. He'd escorted wealthy, elderly ladies all his life and had been something of a lounge lizard. He was one of the few men I knew who actually wore a corset to keep his tummy slim. He'd foxtrot around the bar with his gentleman friend in a world of his own.

BUCK: The St Albans club was a lovely old club. We used to call it the Wrinkle Room, because there were all these wrinkled old gentlemen in there with their young boys. They had more millionaire members of that club than any other club I could think of. And when it closed they all disappeared. And no-one ever found out where they went to, there was just nothing left for them.

JAMES: There was the St Albans Club, which was a smart hotel, very much cocktail bar type, middle to upper-class, elderly, respectable people, who just happened to be gay. And a few doors away in a basement, the Regency Club, which was very much a working-class club. I would say the clientele was a third lesbian, a third gay men and a third straight but everybody was quite, quite happy. It was very working class, you'd get bus drivers of both or all three persuasions. It was only, really, a very large basement living room, as it were, with a bar at the end. There was room for a small dancefloor, probably twelve feet by twelve feet, something like that and no-one would turn a hair at two boys dancing or two girls or a boy and a girl. No-one seemed to bother at all, quite, quite amazing. One of the friendliest clubs I'd ever known, certainly not an exploiting club. The proprietor was most generous with buffets and things for anyone's birthday. He was also regularly tapped for a loan by people who didn't always pay back. Just a nice, kindly uncle figure.

PETER: You could dance in the clubs if they had a disco. It wasn't called a disco in those days, it was a dance area — it was a little postage stamp square and you had to be very careful, you had to be very discreet. If the police happened to visit one of the clubs and there was all men dancing together it wouldn't have been accepted and next time the licence came up for renewal the police would object to it.

SIOBHAN: It was like a round of going from place to place, visiting Brighton. I was never in a big club, I was always in these little tiny places that were like people's lounges. You'd go down into them and there'd be a little bar in the corner and you'd just all sit there and drink until you got drunk and then you'd move on to someone else's. And they were all the same, these little clubs, loads of them! I always felt younger than a lot of people, a lot of them would have been a lot older than me. We were very young. There was a right old mixture of people in them but it wasn't rough, I never saw any trouble.

SANDIE: There was a real sense of comradeship then; you know, 'We're all in this together and let's make the best of it. Let's have fun, make a joke of it.' And there was a song around at that time, we used to go trotting through all those little lanes in Brighton, the little twittens, we used to go, two o'clock in the morning, running down those little lanes, singing, 'Frankfurter sandwiches, frankfurter sandwiches.' You know, the boys and the girls together. And other daft things we did. But oh, it was fun. It was harmless fun, too. In the sixties, there was more of a sort of family feeling. I don't know how else to express it. Because we used to say, then, 'Oh, he's family or she's family.' That was an expression that used to be used then, meaning, 'That's another gay person.' Even if you didn't know them. And that immediately gave you a feeling of closeness because being gay was being one of a minority group.

JO: I don't know what it is but I know, as you go past the Sussex and there's a cinema on the left and then there's this street and you go down that street and then somehow it finishes up at the beach, well, it was in that street there, the Curtain. And there was all sorts of old women come down to Brighton — old lesbians that were, I suppose, ten years older than my age group — who, after the war, were old enough and substantial enough, and got gratuities from the forces and also a lot of them, for some reason, lost their fathers who left them money, and they came down here and bought places and let rooms off. And they always had a gin thing in those days and they used to say they rented the rooms off to people so they could buy bottles of gin. They were all right alcoholics. And they were always in these pubs, they always slurred, 'Hello, my dear.' They were sort of leftovers from Chelsea. I'd met them all in the Gateways, years before, before Sister George, and all these sort of Chelsea ladies used to use the Gateways then. There was one called Kay, there was another one called Krina, and as I say, they were all terribly old, must have been about forty, and they all came down to Brighton to wallow in their gin bottles and get money from their lodgers.

TED: I remember one night at the Curtain Club when they had a fight... This big, butch sailor decides he's gonna lam into one of the queans 'cause he's not getting what he wants. Well, the quean laid him out of course, didn't she? You should have seen it, dear, they were carrying this butch omi out on the stretcher and there's she, standing waving her handbag like a demented windmill saying, 'THE COW, THE COW!'

> **My God, the Sunday mornings we've crept out from under a stone! It's amazing that some of us are still alive, really is.**
> GRANT

Top left Jo and girlfriend, Brighton station photobooth.
Above Jo and two girlfriends!
Top right Gill (far right), Jess and friends on their way to the Variety Club.
Right Friends of Jo, on a day trip.

AILEEN: We went to the Curtain Club once and we never went again. There was a strange sort of feeling. It was like hitting a brick wall and you weren't allowed to go any further. We went there with two of our friends, George and Steve. They took us down there. And I never felt such resentment regarding any females being there. It was as if, this is our sanctum, you're not allowed into it. And I felt rather sad about that because being part of the gay scene, with the Spotted Dog, accepted there, coming up against this barrier, it sort of throws you.

SHEILA: Early sixties, Big Kay as we called her, she tried to open a private club. Jacaranda it was called and it had a private opening night party. There was no drinks allowed, you see, they weren't allowed to sell them. But we were, naturally, having drinks but it was terribly unofficial. They'd only been charging, I think, a shilling for a drink, but they had been charging. And to our horror, the police raided us. Well, I think we all wanted to be violently sick. They didn't arrest anybody, but they walked through the rooms and you can imagine what sort of expression they had on their faces, to see all the girls there, all dressed up. The couples were dancing, and all of a sudden somebody said, 'The police have come.' And I think everybody just stood stock still. I think all our stomachs were churning over like mad. And I think everybody tried to disappear into the darkness. I think that we all tried to appear that we weren't even there, still standing in couples, just waiting. And thank goodness, Kay dealt with the situation and the police went away. It was closed down unfortunately. Which was a great pity, because that would have been the one and only all-girls club. Most of the other places were mixed, which isn't too bad, but then the boys don't always like the girls, and the girls don't always like the boys.

SANDIE: There was quite a lot of intolerance around then because I remember one of the girls who was quite wealthy, an older woman, decided she wanted to open a club and she got fabulous basement premises and we worked like billyho on this place because we were friends of hers. I'm quite artistic and she'd got a games room at the back, and I spent hours painting murals on the walls and in the loo and places like that. She poured a hell of a lot of money into it. But anyway she was daft enough to decide to have a party before she actually got the licence and half way through this party, which was crammed with gay people, I mean there must have been hundreds of us crammed in there, the police arrived and they demanded that all music must be turned off and we all stood perfectly still. And there we had to stand and this team of policemen walked round, like seeing something out of a film, like the gestapo, because the man in charge of this group of policemen had a flat hat on and he had a cane in his hand and he was cracking it against his thigh. And as he walked round, he'd stand in front of us, staring in our faces, looking at everybody and then they all stalked out. I mean there was nothing they could do because we weren't doing anything wrong and it was a private party. But she never got her licence.

PETER: I'd always liked women's company. I've always had a lot of women around me and one or two women in my younger days have

> There was a time when the police were a load of shit. It came to the point where, if they hadn't got anything in the book at the end of the week, they'd bloody well go out and pull in somebody in a cottage or a prostitute from Cannon Place. GRANT

fallen in love with me and it was a job to fight them off — in some cases. In a couple of cases I've even had to tell them 'You're wasting your time, dear, you've got the wrong sort of organ.' And they just laughed and joked about it. I've treated women with respect, which I find some of the gay people don't, and that is wrong, that is totally wrong. It's very bigoted, that and it's very narrow to think in that direction.

VICKY: Going back, God, many, many years, Jean and I wanted to buy a club and I don't know where we were living, we must have been living in Essex. And we'd heard about the Queen's Club coming up for sale, it was on the market, so we decided to go after it and we came to Brighton. It was a men only club. It had gambling rights, it had gambling machine rights. Well, we walked through this club full of men and you could have heard a cigarette drop on the floor. It came to an absolute silent standstill. Cards poised, you know, dice in mid-air! Women in *their* club! Would they ever get over it? Anyway, we went through to this chap's office, oh, he was a slimy sod. I didn't like him at all. Well, we were interested in buying it but they would only let us see his books if we signed the contract. And, of course, I wouldn't sign a contract until I'd seen the books.

It was a pity. I've always wanted a women only club that did everything: that was open all day; that sold coffee; that was a meeting place; a get together for anything; that had music in the evening that you could dance to. I don't know, I mean I'm never going to do it now, I suppose, but I've always wanted to.

HELEN: I used to live with my mother in Eastbourne then and I got rather bored all the time with, shall we say, the establishment life. I thought, 'Is there nothing beyond this forever? Is it always going to be like this?' Occasionally one went down to Brighton. An actor friend used to say, 'Oh, I'll take you round the gay clubs of Brighton, darling.' And he did. And it was all for the men, wasn't it! Round the Greyhound and the Sussex and the 42 Club and it was all chaps. Never met a soul.

Contemporary advertisement.

after the show
Joyce Golding & Ray Jacobs
welcome you at

the queen of clubs

25 bedford square
brighton 1
telephone 775049

open till midnight

MARGARET: The Queen of Clubs was a small place with a very tiny dancing area, just a drinking bar that had music, I suppose that would be records. And at the same time we heard of another one on the seafront and it was in the British Legion Club, I think, 76 Marine Parade it was. Somebody said if you go down to the British Legion Club on a Friday night, gay women take it over or have it for the evening. So then we started coming down to Brighton on a Friday after work to go to this place. Now that place was the best place of all. Because when you went in the drinking clubs there was an element of rough, tough girls but these were more sort of professional. They seemed to be nicer types of people that went to the British Legion Club. It was only on a Friday night, and they were really nice, very friendly. You could have a drink, coffee, dance — that must have had a juke-box — just sit and chat, and then the fellow that ran it closed and moved, moved to Hastings. And that was the end of the British Legion Club.

We found there was another club in Regency Square, called the Regency, so we went round to the Regency, joined that and went down there. That was mixed. The only one that was all female was the British Legion in Marine

Parade and I think that's why we liked it best, because it was all women.

AILEEN: Oh boy, did I love it! Absolutely adored it. Every Saturday night. I couldn't wait for this Queen of Clubs. It was the freedom to be what you are without having to worry about anybody looking at you. You could relax, enjoy, talk, see other people, speak to them, strike up a relationship and it was wonderful. I loved it. It was great, it was exciting, oh, it was a new life.

HARRIET: The Queen of Clubs was mainly women. There were a few men but very few, really. At least it was nice and bright and it was above ground. It was fairly cheerful. They had lights on and it wasn't all dingy and sort of under cover, I didn't like that.

SANDIE: I think the Queen of Clubs was a bit sleazy. I remember the decor wasn't very brilliant and the carpet always seemed to be very sticky. I think that was because the owners of gay clubs could get away with letting the decor go downhill. Gay clubs were few and far between and they knew that their clientele was always going to come in because it was the only place we had to go.

VALERIE: I used to go to the Queen of Clubs with friends. It was quite nice but to me it wasn't quite like the London clubs, it was much sort of quieter and I was surprised to find a lot of older people there, which you tend not to find in the London clubs and I always felt a little bit out of it because everybody knew everybody else. I eventually got to know some of the people there and used to end up on visiting terms with them. But it was much more like a social gathering than anything else, whereas the London clubs tended to have much more of an accent on dancing and picking people up and that sort of thing.

♥   ♥   ♥

JOCELYN: A very butch little number came up to me and said, 'I'd like to ask you to dance but first of all I must know whether you are butch or fem.' I said, 'It depends on who I'm in bed with!' It was very much a divided thing. I always found that a bit strange. I thought, you know, you were both women, that's what it's all about — you're not pretending to be a man. But there were a lot of them about like that who used to wear collars and ties and little suits and be very, very butch and say, 'Don't you look at anyone else while you are dancing with me.' And fem little girlfriends in peep-toed slingbacks and skirts.

SANDIE: There was very much a butch walk and a butch way of sitting. You didn't cross your legs if you were butch, you sat there with your knees apart and you rested your elbows on your knees. Or when you crossed your legs, you crossed your ankle over your knee. And butch meant being the one that always went up to the counter in the club or the pub and butch meant having the money and paying for the drinks. Funny, though, I think it was a little bit like men and women tend to be. It was often the fem one who made all the decisions at home. I think the purse strings were really held by the feminine one rather than the butch one.

BOBBY: I used to dress up more like a butch person. Sometimes I'd wear ties and things, adopt the mannerisms more of young men than young women. You know, offering people cigarettes and buying people drinks and opening doors for them and letting them sit down if there was only one seat and that kind of thing. Very gentlemanly.

HARRIET: Some of the butch women used to make awful remarks: 'The wife's at home cooking lunch' or something and it was absolutely appalling. It must have been like being married to a man, if you're going to put up with that nonsense. One of them, tiny little thing always used to wear bow ties and trousers and collars and shirts and everything. She even used to wear little Y-fronts.

JAN: There were women that wore suits and ties, really close-cropped hairstyles. I used to wear trousers and a shirt and a sweater and what have you but I never tried to hide the fact that I'd got breasts — and they are quite ample, you know. But I know a lot of women did, they tried to hide the fact. That's what shocked me, I think, coming to Brighton, that women were trying to disguise the fact that they were women. The way I feel is that if I'd wanted a man, I'd have one, not a substitute. I like women and I am very much a woman.

SANDIE: There were never really enough feminine women to go round. Feminine women were always in very short supply. There were far more butch ones around. But maybe that's what's led to what's happened today, with everybody looking neither one thing nor the other. I mean in those days, you used to say, 'Oh, she doesn't know whether she's Arthur or Martha.'

JO: I used to get a kick out of going with straight girls but I used to get some of them say, 'If it ever struck me that you were a woman, I'd be sick.' I've had that said to me and then women that were embarrassed going out with me, in case people realised I was a woman. But I didn't try to con them into believing I was a real man. No way. I mean, I used to get away with it if I picked up a woman that didn't know I was gay and I'd see her home and kiss her goodnight and I'd never see her again. Then I'd get a big sort of high from it. But I could never have followed it up because, I mean, what would you do?

SANDIE: After all, being butch is a kind of act you can only keep up some of the time. Because when you're at home, in the basic sort of everyday living with a woman, however masculine she is, she's still a woman. She's still going to have her periods, you know, and bellyache sometimes and all that sort of thing. She can't avoid all of that, she's got to be a woman at some point. The act has to be dropped sometimes.

BOBBY: I enjoyed playing the male part, asking someone if they'd like to dance or if they'd like a drink. You know, the chatting up bit. I enjoyed doing that. My friend enjoyed talking to people. Probably not with the same sexual interest that I had. I mean, I was very excited by people that wore make-up and short skirts. I don't think she was. I think that I had always wanted to be male rather than female. I used to dislike my body, very much so. I've given up now, but I did dislike it and I wanted to be masculine and muscular. I hated the breasts growing and so on and I hated it when I started a period and things. So it was a total rejection of my body, I think. But I certainly wouldn't have done anything about it. I saw a TV programme recently about a woman who had a sex change. I don't think I could have gone into all that.

♥   ♥   ♥

SHEILA: In the country, with the motorbike, it was so handy because you could go all over the place. You could spend the day riding round and then you'd sit and smooch — you couldn't do it in public — and if anybody walked nearby they would probably think you were just an ordinary couple. I was always dressed up in my gear, you see, in my boots and my slacks and my helmet, 'course nobody knew any difference, so we could be quite blasé, have a snogging session in Newtimber, that was quite exciting. You could walk sort of hand in hand, I had my hair cut quite short and, as I say, with my outfit on, it was difficult to tell I was a woman. You wouldn't be too blatant but I think it was the fact that you were doing it that made it a little element of danger. Set the old blood racing — being daring, I suppose. And of course, sitting on the bike, get a nice little squeeze from the back.

I know once we went out in the country and we both came back bitten from top to bottom with mosquito bites. It was all marshy out Newtimber way and we came back, we undressed, we were bitten all over. It was pretty embarrassing because we were both bitten in the same places!

JOCELYN: I mean, I was completely bowled over by the whole thing. There was me discovering about sex at the age of thirty in a very, very wonderful way. I was absolutely bowled over by the whole thing.

SANDIE: I can only speak for myself and other people's experience might, perhaps, be totally different. My experience was that once you undressed a butch woman, she wasn't a butch woman any longer. Obviously, there were exceptions to that rule but I've always had a fairly strong personality, without being masculine and frequently I found myself taking the lead. I liked a woman to look more masculine than I was but I never expected a woman to be anything but a woman, when it came down to it. I love women because they're women, not because they take off men.

VICKY: At one point, I wouldn't let anyone touch me. Jean never touched me. So I didn't know what a climax was till I was twenty-eight. I didn't even know what masturbation was. I didn't know how to do it. When I did know what it was all about and actually got into a relationship that was a two-way thing, I thought about all the years that I'd wasted — which wasn't

> **66** Well, my mother did offer me money to go and have a sex change. GILL **99**

81

a waste really, because I'd loved Jean. I'd loved Jean more than anything else in the world. So it hadn't been a waste but I feel that there were aspects of it that could have been improved.

BOBBY: My first relationship was wonderful, simply on the sexual level because I hadn't ever been able to express those sorts of feelings before. I thought it was fantastic. It was a tremendous release and it was very good. Now, the woman I was having this affair with was quite experienced, in a sense. She was not riddled with the sort of guilt that I was riddled with and she was also capable of having a boyfriend at the same time so it wasn't a kind of living together relationship, it was simply a friendship which had sexual tones when we wanted it to.

ANNIE: I was never any good with men in bed. Hopeless. I didn't try very often. But it was a dead loss. Didn't enjoy it, just thought, you know, 'What the hell's this about?' But it wasn't any problem with women. Always seemed to work very nicely.

SHEILA: I did go out with one or two chaps. But it never seemed right. It seemed all wrong to me. I've never been with a man sexually. I didn't get roused. I could get attracted to a woman that way and it felt right, me making love to a woman, but it didn't feel a bit right with a man making love to me. So, I think then I knew that I could never, ever have a serious relationship with a man because I could never, ever let him make love to me. It just didn't seem that it was the right thing to do. So, I think then that I knew that I wasn't like other women.

SANDIE: We must have known the word dyke, actually, because we lived in Dyke Road and we always thought that was hysterical. So the word 'dyke' was familiar but we didn't really associate it with ourselves. It was something that American lesbians were called.

JANICE: Now Brighton, from my recollection, was a lot worse for fights than London. You'd get these real, butch dykes, these real diesel jobs, you know, big, who thought they were all boxing champion types. And they were always fighting. I never got involved in any fights. I took care to wear something ultra feminine down to Brighton because that way you'd be left alone. You see, they'd never dream of hitting a lady. They behaved the way they thought men did. 'Course, men never have behaved like that really but they thought they did. So it went with the territory, with the Y-fronts, you know.

SANDIE: Of course the butch girls were very much more obvious. And because of that I think they had to have a lot more courage. They were not as easily accepted by society as a whole, so they had to have a lot more bravado and courage to go out and face the world. And it used to get you into some sticky situations. I remember, I don't know if it still exists, but there was this bar, the Belvedere along Brighton seafront, underneath the arches and sometimes some of the girls used to go in there, and so did sailors and people like that. Well, we went in this bar one night, my girlfriend and I, and I expect one or two others. There were some sailors in there who'd been

Top left Private party, mid-fifties.
Left Ready to go out, Saturday night, 1962, Vicky and friends.
Above Sixties lesbian chic.

drinking, and one of them got stroppy and started to have a go at my girlfriend and she must have been quaking in her shoes because he was a great, beefy, muscular character, you know, and he was really quite aggressive. He was standing there and swaying around and threatening her and swinging his fists around and telling her what he was planning to do to her . . . And I jumped up, in all my feminine clothes and I stood between him and her and I said, 'Over my dead body you will!' One of his mates came up and said, 'Come on, leave the lesbians alone.' And they walked away, so that was lucky.

VICKY: No-one could ever call Jean timid. If ever I was in trouble, I'd certainly want Jean behind me. She was extremely good if anyone ever threatened me. I mean, I was a tearaway then. I used to get into all kinds of trouble 'cause I've got a very short fuse. There could be a burst of, 'Don't talk to my girl!'

SANDIE: Butch girls had to be courageous because, of course, they sometimes needed to go into public toilets. Well, when they'd got all this gear on, going into the ladies toilet, naturally sometimes they were challenged by straight women who were going in there, 'Oh, you're in the wrong toilet!' And certainly, my girlfriend used to pull her jacket back, flash her boobs and say, 'It's alright, darling!' Or she'd stand in the doorway and say, 'This way to the Laddies!' Oh dear, yes. They had a lot of courage and they were great fun.

SHEILA: I had a black shirt and a very slim white tie and trousers. We had to be careful because if you were walking in a group, you used to have the mickey taken out of you. When you got off the bus on your way to a pub or going from one club to another, you'd be walking down, looking in shop windows and things like that, and get a little bit blasé. You'd get comments made as people went by, mostly chaps. There was always somebody that would shout out, 'Load of dykes!'

SANDIE: I don't mind being called a lesbian now but it's never been my favourite word, I must say. And it was an absolutely taboo word years ago, which is probably why I find it difficult to use now. To me, it was an insult, you see. It was definitely used as an insult. To be called a 'Les', which is what straight people always used to say, 'Les be friends' used to be a stupid joke, you know.

JANINE: I remember being shouted at on a train going up to Victoria and going to meet some friends at the Gateways and sitting in a carriage all by myself. I must have been nineteen, twenty, twenty-one, something like that and there were some youths shouting out, 'She's a bloody lesbian!' or something and being very, very upset by this. It was this strange dichotomy, I don't want to go on about Public Schools but that kind of sheltered upbringing, into the WRAC for three years and then making my own life and it was very difficult to marry the two up, and being gay on top of it all was another, not difficulty, but it meant sort of constant adjustment.

SANDIE: I think Brighton was one of the most accepting places, because there were so many of the boys there and it was publicly known among straight as well as gay people as the gay Mecca of the South Coast, people almost expected to come to Brighton and see gays. I think it was more acceptable than it was anywhere else. In other places it was totally unacceptable. We got smutty remarks you know, whatever they could turn their puerile minds to. But on the whole they didn't go into the attack. Mainly, of course, because it was men against women and back in the sixties that was still unacceptable, basically, for a man to beat up a woman. I think a fair amount of the boys got beaten up in those days. But no, it was a fairly rare thing with women.

There was a girl called Noddy, though, who came out of the army. Noddy, that was a lovely name, isn't it? Came out of the army and moved to Brighton. Don't think she'd ever met any real prejudice. She came from Newcastle. She'd got a wonderful Geordie accent, fascinating. She was a good-looking girl too. I rather liked her . . . Anyway that was a long time ago. But she was very butch and dressed very butch and, unfortunately for her, she was walking home on her own through Brighton one night, and there was a gang of lads and I don't know if they'd seen where she'd left, you know, if she'd left a club that they recognised as a gay club or what, but they chased her through Brighton. She was fairly fit and ran as well as she could to get away from them, but when you're up against a gang of five or six, it's very unfair odds and they caught up with her in a little churchyard just off the road up to the station, Queens Road, and they beat the daylights out of her. She was black and blue. And that was just prejudice. Nothing else.

We were figures of fun, I daresay, as much as anything. People used to stare and then they turned to their straight friends and there'd be a whispered conversation and then roars of laughter so you can imagine the sort of smutty remarks that were going round the straight group. But, I mean, we were very thick skinned, we learnt to ignore that. We expected that, that was typical of the sixties, that sort of prejudice.

♥   ♥   ♥

MARGARET: It was 1964. One of Eve's jobs at work was to go through all the newspapers every single day and cut out anything to do with the Midland Bank. It had to be stuck into scrapbooks or something. And she must have read through the papers as well, because she came home having cut out all the personal adverts. She said, 'I want you to look at this advert. I can't believe it, I saw it in The Times today.' I can't remember the exact wording of it but it said, 'Homosexual women meet at the Shakespeare's Head, Carnaby Street, on such and such a date.' And she said, 'What do you think about this, shall we go?' And I said, 'We can't, we can't go up there.' So she said, 'Let's go.' So when this date came along we went and found Carnaby Street and we went and looked at this Shakespeare's Head and it looked a bit tatty. And we walked up and down outside, looking at this place, and I said, 'I'm not going in there.' And she said, 'No, no, I'm not going in there either.' So we went back home wondering what it was all about. So I said, 'Well, keep an eye in case there's another advert and maybe we'll

> **"** If you were out walking and you went arm in arm, dear oh dear, that was very daring, it was for me anyway. SHEILA **"**

Arena Three

From Arena Three, magazine of the Minorities Research Group.

pluck up courage at some time to go into this place.' So anyway, a few weeks later there was another advert: 'Homosexual women meeting at the upstairs bar at the Shakespeare's Head.' So we went up there again and we walked up and down outside and then we saw a girl go in and walk up the stairs. She was a bit more confident than me. She said, 'Come on,' she said, 'You follow me.' And so we walked up the stairs and we went into this room and there were about forty women, I suppose, in this room. There was a girl on the door and she asked us our names and we told her and so she said, 'Oh, it's nice of you to come and to turn up.' And everybody was sitting at little tables, four at a table, and so she said, 'As you won't know anybody, I'll put you on a table with two other new people.' She said, 'We get new people every time.'

BARBARA: Minorities Research Group it was called, based in London. It was in the national press, I think. It certainly wasn't by word of mouth that I knew about it. I just barged into this place one evening and introduced myself and God, it was a crowd! I had written and they said, 'Come up for a meeting.' They met monthly in a pub just behind Liberty's, off Regent Street. It was a little social evening, you see, you went up once a month for this social do, and you met and all chatted and talked and it was really, really lovely. I was very impressed. And when they asked for a representative for the South Coast, I stood up and said I'd take it on.

MARGARET: After about three or four months, too many women started going to the Shakepeare's Head, it became too small, they had to find another place for us to go and they found the Bull's Head, I think it was called, at Clapham. One of the speakers was Bryan Magee and he came along one evening and he said he was writing a book called, 'One in Twenty' and he'd been to male homosexual clubs and he'd interviewed men and he wanted to interview a few of the women for his book. But there was only this one meeting a month and the numbers were getting greater and greater, 100 to 150 by now. So Esme Langley and her girlfriend, Diana Chapman, who were in charge, decided that they would have to split this group, which was called MRG, into four and they would split it sort of north east, north west, and the Clapham part would be the south west London and Surrey group.

BARBARA: Then they would write to me from London, if it fell between the meetings that somebody wanted to be seen or wanted me to visit them or wanted help or wanted to come and see me. They would write to me or phone me. One just said, 'Well, we're having a little get together on Friday, would you like to come and meet everybody? Or would you like to come first on your own and perhaps see me? Or would you like me to come and visit you?' Often they wanted us to go there and with Joan having a car and loving driving, we zoomed along the coast and in the countryside, visiting these lesbians who were heartbroken or who'd parted or were having rows and Joan would drive off somewhere or sit in the background whilst I was listening or seeing how I could help.

There was a very young one, very young one, she was a nurse. She was in love with a sister and carrying on with her and then the sister must

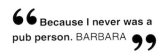
have seen the danger point and left her to go off with another sister. So this kid was absolutely bereft, she was going berserk, in fact she did have a breakdown. And I don't know where she'd heard of the MRG but she just phoned, she had my number, everybody knew my number, it wasn't private.

There were two that lived just outside Eastbourne. They had a caravan, a Romany caravan and they had a donkey. Oh, I used to think it was heaven going there and the village in the springtime was filled with snowdrops. I liked going there and they were lovely people, too. I don't think they knew anybody else, only us. But we would go there and have little tea parties on the lawn. It was wonderful to go to these things because you could just be yourself, you hadn't to pretend or be afraid to make a glance or a gesture or say what you thought. It was wonderful to be free and I think the MRG, I think they did a damned good job.

There were never more than eight of us. Eight or nine, maybe ten on occasions. I remember once we met on the beach at Worthing and we took some fish, mackerel or something quite humble, and we cooked them on an open fire, collecting bits of wood and we made a fire like a lot of little girl guides. Well, you know, if you've got children with you, you can get away with this, can't you, making fires on the beach. But a little gang of middle aged, well not middle aged, thirties women, doing this, I suppose people looking at us thought we were quite cranky. But we enjoyed it.

There was this funny one, I call her a funny one, not with disrespect, she just really made me laugh to look at her. She was very short and stocky and butch and screamed lesbian, I am a lesbian, you know it screamed from her. I mean, she was a very big-hearted girl and sentimental, soft as a puppy. She lived in a caravan, an ordinary caravan. So when it was her turn to have us to visit her, we all squashed into this caravan. You couldn't dance, it was too tiny but I suppose we used to tell what we thought were dirty jokes or daring jokes or risky jokes and stories and tell of our experiences and discuss things quite openly. I suppose it was like being in the psychiatrist's chair, really, so good for us all.

We would do the rounds. But our house seemed to be the base where they could always come at any time. They could ring up and come if they wanted to. And we used to periodically put on these dos, oh, they were lovely. We'd say to the neighbours, 'Oh, I'm having a party tonight, we might be making a bit of noise but come and join us. If you can't beat us, join us.' The wife, oh, she was lovely, she'd say, 'Oh, flow in to me for coffee, you can't cope with all that lot for coffee.' And she never intruded but she was always there, she knew. And never, never openly discussed. But it was so obvious.

The MRG fizzled out after about three years. It didn't last very long. I think it was about three years because there was jealousy and competition in the hierarchy. And I think there was a splinter group. It broke away because they didn't agree with all their activities. It did fall apart soon after that which was a pity. Because there wasn't the centre in London. There was nobody to get in touch with, as it were. It wasn't here today and gone tomorrow, it sort of fizzled out. We gradually stopped having our social functions around Brighton.

M ARGARET: I think the MRG were still having one large meeting at the Bull's Head but when they split us into the smaller groups, we wanted

Bryan Magee's 'sympathetic account of a difficult subject,' 1969.

more social activities. Anyway, when we went to these people's house in Kew somebody suggested that we form another group. We didn't want to be part of this MRG. Let's make ourselves into another group, a social group, so that we went round to people's houses and we had coffees and we went out for rambles or whatever and we weren't part of this big group. So all the people that were there were in favour and she said, 'Well, what shall we call ourselves?' So lots of people had different names, lots of people had different ideas, and these two ladies whose house we were in were near enough to Richmond. And a few of the other people came from Kensington. So they decided they'd put the two together and they'd have Kensington and Richmond. It was too big, Kensington and Richmond so we'll cut it down, so we'll have it Ken and Ric. So we called ourselves Kenric and we formed a committee. I was the first treasurer. It's still going and it's got about 1,500 members and it started with twenty-five in 1965.

❤   ❤   ❤

JANICE: Everything was fun then, really. You've got to remember that in the sixties, everything was new, wasn't it? Everything hadn't been done before and certainly, from the lesbian point of view, it was the start of a whole new era for lesbians to actually come out as being like that, more so than ever. But to do something as controversial as 'The Killing of Sister George' then — although now it seems very dated and quite amusing — it was very brave, actually, very brave. And brave for the people who were in it.

SHEILA: We used to go to the pictures more often then, well, I used to, anyway. Pictures were quite good in those days. I mean, you had two pictures plus all the little pictures and you could sit and see the film round again, if you liked. And you could hold hands underneath your coats, that was exciting. Sort of look all around and pretend that you were just sitting watching the film and you were getting all hot under the collar.

GEORGE: I remember going to the Gaiety in the Lewes Road, which was the dirty cinema in those days, you didn't go to the Gaiety unless you wanted to see a dirty film. And they'd got 'Victim' on, Dirk Bogarde film. And I remember being very moved by it, it touched nerves within me, you know? I mean, I didn't comprehend the blackmail thing because it had never happened to me but I remember the young boy being infatuated with the older man and I remember the shock of the garage door coming down and it had got 'QUEER' written on it.

JAMES: There was a lovely film, I think of Dutch or Scandinavian origin, about a teenage boy who was gay and his parents had bribed the au pair to seduce him to make him straight, or something. And the teenage boy's grown-up admirer took a court case against the parents for sexually seducing a minor. I can't remember the name of the film but it played, I think, at the Paris in New Road. And there was great applause and 'Hurray!' at the end because it was most unusual. Even today, that would be unusual.

> 66 I used to like going watching Soldiers in Skirts. Oh, they were fantastic. I used to always go and see their shows. SHEILA 99

Top left On the beach at Black Rock.
Left On a boat from Palace Pier.
Top right Jo shinning up a lamp-post.
Above Sandie and girlfriend.

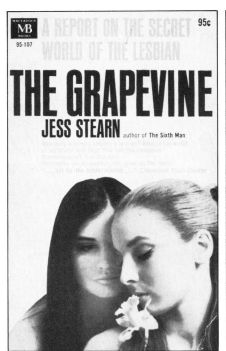

'They were passed from hand to hand.'
Lesbian and gay publications of the fifties and sixties.

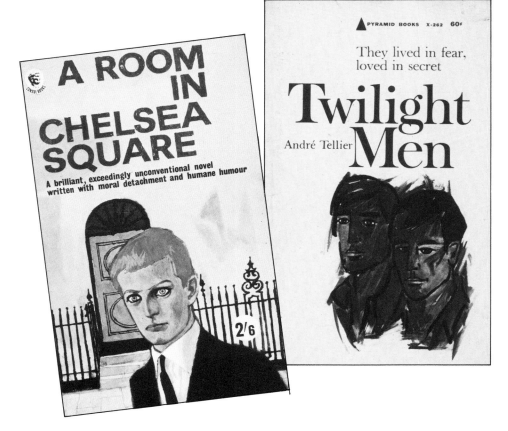

PATRICK: I would be about twelve, thirteen, when I discovered the Unicorn bookshop in Gloucester Road. It was what they called in those days an underground bookshop. Bill Butler ran this one and he was a very great American poet, a great intellectual, an enormously larger than life man. He was about six foot seven, he looked like John Wayne and lived with his lover. No-one would ever have thought, for a second, that he was gay. He used to wear a great big stetson hat and had a wicked sense of humour. We'd sell the ordinary books like, 'The Naked Lunch', 'The Politics of Ecstasy' and things like that, but we'd always throw in a couple of gay books as well. It was amazing, the number of people that used to write in for 'City of Night' by John Rechy or 'Numbers' or something like that. They might put a little PS and say, 'Do you have any more books of the same type?' In other words, they were screaming old queans who wanted more gay books. We used to recommend 'Our Lady of the Flowers' and 'Funeral Rites' by Genet. But in North Road, there was what they used to call a dirty bookshop, which you'll never find now, where everything was cellophane wrapped and they would have all these ghastly books in the window. 'Miss Whiplash' and all that sort of thing. But there'd always be one in the middle which would be a lurid gay book with a terrible piece written on the back saying, 'Brad and Jed were two men from another world and their lust for each other caused them to fall into a cesspit of whirling, unnatural desire.' And then the last line would always be, '. . . and finally, they paid the price', which meant that one of them committed suicide because in any lurid gay novel, one of them had to commit suicide. It had to be shown that it was an unnatural lust. But we didn't really sell those at the Unicorn, no, we were a bit upmarket with our gay books. It really was Genet and Burroughs and things like that. But we used to get dirty old men coming in, thinking that 'The Naked Lunch' was going to give them a good time for a toss off and then, of course, they'd read it and they couldn't understand a fucking word.

JAMES: Boots in Western Road — where Virgin Records and McDonalds now are — was a fabulous building, several floors, including at one time, a restaurant with a small band playing. Three lovely, eccentric ladies played piano, fiddle and 'cello. There was a lad called Michael who managed the book department. He used to keep a shelf full of naughty novels. They'd be terribly, terribly tame these days, things like Mary Renault; he would get the very latest and gentlemen would go in, very discreetly, and say, 'Is there anything new in?' And he would say, 'Well, if you just look up there, the one with the pink cover, I think you might find it interesting.'

ARTHUR: The definite, definite gay books, I suppose the first one was 'Quatrefoil', which I thought was beautiful and so sad. In fact, I was reading it in bed and we had separate rooms in that flat and I was so moved by it, I went to see if my partner, Colin, was still alright. I had to look to see him sleeping. I thought, 'Oh, he's alright. I can go to sleep now.'

DENNIS: The first gay book I ever read was called 'Finistère' by Fritz Peters. I read that when I was in the army. I read about it in the New Statesman which used to give reviews on anything a bit naughty like that. I got the New Statesman for years in the hope of finding out more books.

PETER: 'Finistère' was a very famous gay book. It's about a French sports master and a love affair he had. It's a lovely story and it has a tear jerking end to it. That was one of the first gay books I ever read. There weren't many about in those days. Books of that type that were near the knuckle were usually banned in this country.

BOBBY: I didn't know about lesbian novels and I didn't want anything to do with that sort of literature, anyway. Must be going back to the old Catholicism again but I would hardly read books of that kind. Friends of mine tried to persuade me to read 'The Well of Loneliness' and I wouldn't. In fact, I didn't read it until about fifteen years ago and then I found it a very moving book. But at first I wouldn't read it because it was a lesbian novel and I didn't want to know.

JAN: 'The Well of Loneliness' — the bible. There was so much I could relate to with Stephen and how I felt as a child and that. I mean, obviously I didn't have such a lonely childhood as she had but there was so much in it, the way she described everything, that I could relate to. That was the only lesbian book that I read at that stage except for a really tacky book which was, 'My Sister, My Bride' but I obviously didn't take it seriously, it really was so tacky.

JANINE: I came across 'The Well of Loneliness' when I was in the WRAC and people were reading it then. Oh, all that purple prose. Rafferty, the horse, Rafferty, God, I was overwhelmed by it. It was so badly written. It's the most appallingly rich, overblown prose. I adored every second of it. She was called Stephen. She called herself Stephen. But her horse died, I'm sure it was called Rafferty. I haven't read it since I was in my twenties. But I remember being terribly excited by it and it was absolutely wonderful. I identified totally with her because I had a horse you know.

'My Sister, My Bride' — 'a novel about two women with strange desires, each racing on a path to inevitable destruction,' 1968.

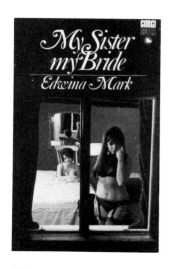

VICKY: I'd heard about this book and I went to the library. When I went and asked for it, I was met with an absolute wall of silence. And I can remember this girl looking at me and saying, 'Oh well, you have to order that book.' Her whole attitude was absolute coldness. You could cut the atmosphere with a knife and I remember going absolutely scarlet and wanting to get out of there as quick as my little legs would carry me. I wasn't even going to go back for it, that's how embarrassed I was. But I did go back and get it and read it. I must have read it about three or four times. I thought it was a wonderful story. It was sad, sad and true and it was good.

♥   ♥   ♥

JANINE: At the time of Wolfenden we were very, very concerned for Michael and Bob and Kevin and Bob and all these people. I don't think that any of my close friends were ever imprisoned but they were terribly aware of it. But it was far more from the male point of view that I was aware of it, 'cause, I mean, Queen Victoria said there's no such thing as lesbianism, it can't exist.

JAMES: Around the time of the Wolfenden Report and things like that I would have shown interest and I subscribed to the Homosexual Law Reform Society which then, because pressure groups cannot be charities, had a parallel organisation called the Albany Trust which did counselling and that sort of thing. As a charity, it could be tax free on subscriptions. They had a very nice illustrated magazine at the time called 'Man and Society' which was a well produced magazine with photographic cover and good articles and things in it. The Director of it was Anthony Grey who was a barrister, and he came down to Brighton with his friend and persuaded the club owners to have a collecting box on the counter at various clubs. He asked me would I go round regularly and empty and send the money on, which I did, for a few years.

JOHN: I was very much involved with the campaign to get law reform. There was the Homosexual Law Reform Society and the Albany Trust running from offices in Shaftesbury Avenue. I was involved on a kind of voluntary work basis. I saw that the chance of law reform was pretty good. And I felt that it needed a lot of backing from people in public life and important places. That was very difficult to get because even if people were gay, they were secretly gay. And famous personalities, public figures, and so on, were secretly gay. They never came out of the closet as we now call it. I made approaches to a number of gay priests in the area and asked them if they would join together in some kind of petition or a campaign, or any kind of an action that we could do to push the law reform a little nearer, and they all refused. Absolutely refused. They just didn't want to know. They were so angry with me for even suggesting that they might be interested.

JANINE: How do I say this without being offensive or sounding offensive, sounds offensive to my ear before I even say it . . . If you were extremely middle class and you were gay and you'd sorted yourself out and you had inherited money and you owned your own house, then you made a circle of friends and it was an extremely selfish life. You didn't think as much as I do now that you needed to support gay causes, I mean they were things, on the whole, that happened to other people and that's a terrible thing to say but that's how it was if I'm honest about it.

VALERIE: The way I summed it up was, the situation I was in, in the WRAF, was the same situation that these men were in, wherever they were, just in life generally, and I felt deeply sorry for them. Society would not allow them to have a normal life. And this drove them to a sort of warped attitude of life, and a lot of them probably couldn't form a stable relationship simply because they were scared to, perhaps because of their job or something like that.

RICHARD: I was very aware of the law changing in 1967. Oh, yes, very much so. Because that made life a bit easier for me, because I always felt that I was living against the law anyway. And that was not just the law of the land, but I also had something of a problem with the fact that it was against God too. I don't now believe that, of course, but in those early days I did. I felt that I was doing something terribly sinful, and I felt, on the other

> 66 We went to a meeting of, I think it was the Homosexual Law Reform Society which did so much wonderful work at the Conway Hall in London. Everyone was sitting like this looking through their fingers and trying not to be bold and blatant, it was terrible! Extraordinary!
> ARTHUR 99

" We were all criminals. There was a bond. And you honoured that bond. Even with people who were foul, people you didn't like. You would stand by them.
JAMES "

side of that, that I hadn't really got a choice because there was a kind of need in me to do it. And I thought I had to respond to that need, I wasn't strong enough to deny myself totally and be celibate. So I just used to think, 'Oh well, perhaps He won't look too badly on me, I've got to do something wrong sometime in my life so it might as well be this.' Because I don't think I've done anything wrong in my life before and I sort of satisfied myself with that, but when the law changed and it was permissible for consenting males in private, then that did ease the burden in my mind somewhat because I then thought, 'Well, you know, if it's being thought about and talked about and obviously church men were involved in all those things, discussions as well, then perhaps it wasn't so terrible after all.'

JAMES: Gay couples who lived together were not hounded; they had it at the back of their minds all the time that they could be shopped, but what they would probably do would be to keep two separate bedrooms made up. If you were living with and sharing a bedroom with another man you were more or less inviting hostile or self-righteous, puritanical neighbours to tell the police that you were habitual criminals, and it wasn't unknown for the police to get a search warrant and come in and look at sheets and things. Particularly if two fellas lived in a house with a double bed and there would have been room for two singles. But generally couples who did live together didn't fear immediate arrest or anything like that and therefore the change in law didn't make much difference, because after all that's all the change in law did, it didn't make anything else legal, cottaging or threesomes or anything involving the armed forces for instance. And when you consider how popular Brighton was for sailors . . . sailors from Portsmouth would come to Brighton to earn a few quid and get a bed for the night or whatever. I felt very pleased, very relieved about the law change but, as I say, I can't remember that we celebrated in any way at all. It was extraordinary really, we just took it to be one of the many advances that were made legally in the sixties, one of the many liberalising pieces of legislation, all moving in the right direction. Strange, isn't it, that I can't remember anything positive about it?

JOHN: I think this was all too much for the police. You know, they couldn't cope with gays having some power, and having a voice and being heard. They still wanted to oppress us and their means of doing it, by homosexuality being totally illegal, had been taken from them. They still were snatching people from cottages. They still had the agent provocateur activities here in Brighton. Kissing in public, even holding hands in public were grossly indecent and not allowed. So, you know, homosexual law reform was only really a very small achievement, by comparison with what we really wanted and what we really should have had. But it was felt at that time that it was better than nothing at all. Occasionally there'd be little sort of groups of police, albeit sometimes plain clothes, even in the nude, strolling along Telscombe beach for example in the hope of catching gay men at sex.

❤   ❤   ❤

JAMES: In London, one could go to certain second-hand paperback bookshops to buy muscle magazines with pictures of half-naked men. They had titles like Man Alive or Physique Pictorial. They were the nearest thing to a gay magazine in the fifties and they would always be on the back shelf, behind the counter. You'd say, 'Could I have that, please?' And some of the newsvendors in London, the street magazine sellers, would have just one among dozens and dozens of 'Women and Home' and 'Ideal Garden' and things like that. But just one. . . You could just see it. And it would be replaced by one from under the counter. It was all very, very discreet. There was nothing anyone could object to in them. They were either painted over or wearing pouches or something. But I remember there was one absolutely god-like creature whose name was Glen Bishop, who used to pose in these things. He was absolutely beautiful as well as muscle-bound.

From Spartacus Magazine.

JOHN: I was the first to publish a magazine in this country which said, 'For homosexuals, about homosexuals, by homosexuals' and I was the first to publish frontal male nude photographs. Let me tell you exactly what happened. I started with sets of photographs, just postcard sized prints. Black and white photographs, mainly not nude, there were some nude sets. And I started by advertising those. I made a little brochure and mailed it out and from that we went on to the magazine. There was, at that time, a magazine called International Times, which was basically a hippy magazine, all the sort of flower power. But they had a males' column in the classifieds and that was just a gay advertising medium. And it was very popular. But the police were persecuting them because of it. And they were very anxious to unload this males column and to get rid of it . . . There was another thing called, 'Films and Filming' which a lot of gay people used to advertise in. I never could understand why. But they suddenly stopped because, again, they were attacked by the authorities. There was another thing which was called 'The International Male Magazine' or TIMM. They never used the word 'gay', they never used the word 'homosexual'. They never admitted to being gay, although it was quite clear that they were a gay publication and it was all about homosexuality. They had photographs of young men, never full frontal. There was always either briefs or a bush with some leaves in front of their dangly bits. There was always something that you couldn't quite see what you were hoping to see. And of course, full frontal male nude photographs were quite illegal in those days. In fact, they were perhaps pushing their luck, doing what they did. But people were dissatisfied with TIMM. They felt it didn't go far enough and they wanted something that went all the way and something that was openly for homosexuals.

I've never been a person to be afraid of doing something. So I had the idea to start a magazine and to give it a title which was quite clumsy but which would tell people that it was replacing these other things. So we called it 'The International Males' Advertiser'. I had a few mailing lists that were sort of gay. There used to be a number of companies that sold swimwear and briefs with nice pictures of good looking guys, modelling these things. And of course, it was quite obvious that they made more money selling their brochures than they did selling their briefs. Clearly, their mailing lists were basically gay mailing lists. Well, I acquired several of those.

The photographs were something that I did on my own. There was a guy called John Barrington, he gave me quite a lot of help in the early days. Then the magazine had various people who would write articles for me, like Peter Burton. We had a woman artist who drew pictures under the name Spartacus because she didn't want to come out as being interested in naked men. And somebody who did the graphic design, a professional designer called Eric Batten, who lived near Seven Dials, who I met over the frozen fish counter in Waitrose supermarket.

The first issue of this magazine came out and, I believe, on the first page we announced, bravely, this magazine was for homosexuals, by homosexuals and about homosexuals and homosexuality. And I remember going around all the sex shops in London and bookstores and so on, literally shaking from head to foot, with a bag full of these magazines. And it was very successful, right from the beginning. We were printing and selling perhaps 3,000 copies.

Around, I think, the sixth issue, the fifth or sixth issue, we changed the name to Spartacus. Spartacus was a slave who got the rough end of the stick from society. And he fought for freedom from oppression, for himself and for other slaves in the same position. And basically, in a parallel kind of way, that's what we were doing. We were fighting for freedom from oppression for gay people. For gay men particularly. There wasn't much consideration about lesbians, just at that time. They were another kind of animal, that we didn't mate with, kind of thing. So we called the thing 'Spartacus'. It also had this nice 'masculine' ring because in the personal advertisements in these various publications, including our own, terms like, 'effeminate types need not apply' or 'masculine types only' were beginning to appear.

So we followed along this same theme in our publication. We had masculine type models. We had stories about male homosexuals. We had articles . . . In the meantime, the law reform had gone through. That was in sixty-seven and we started, perhaps in sixty-eight or sixty-nine, I'm not quite sure. It was a brave move. We were persecuted. We were frequently visited by a police officer that hoped somehow to stop us. But we weren't actually doing anything that was illegal. There was no law that said you can't publish magazines about homosexuality. There was no law that said homosexuals can't be organised in groups.

Now, our magazine started, I guess, half a year before the Gay Liberation Front started. That started with the Stonewall riots in New York. And half a year before that, in our Spartacus magazine, I was writing, 'It's time that gay men stood up and were counted.' And pointing out that if all the gay doctors and gay teachers were to admit to being gay, they couldn't fire them all because the medical service and the educational service would grind to a halt. And the same in all other professions. There was no profession which could risk firing all its gay members. So what was there to be afraid of ? I mean, if we all do it, as a community, there's nothing to be afraid of. And I was the first one to actually put this idea into print. And it was very widely read.

EDWARD: I discovered Spartacus, I don't know quite how but I was intrigued by this because the only kind of magazines one could see in those days were naturist things called, I think, 'Health and Efficiency' or 'Health and Strength' and I found those exciting enough, I suppose, at the

From Spartacus Magazine.

ODD MAN OUT by ROGER FARLEIGH

time. Anyway, you could buy them at Smiths and they were on the top shelf, you had to reach for them, slightly coy if you did buy one, of course. But I found them quite fun. You'd find pages of dad and mum and the children, all playing tennis with no clothes on, which I suppose was interesting enough. But when this thing called Spartacus appeared I wrote for a copy of that. It was in Preston Street and seeing an advertisement I then decided the thing to do was to come down and buy a copy because I couldn't trust the post. Obviously, somebody would find out that I was gay. So when I was here one day, I found Preston Street and to my astonishment, there was a little shop window, which seemed to be full of leather jock straps and things like that which I hadn't seen displayed in public before. Went in, upstairs room and said, 'Could I buy a copy of Spartacus?' And did. It was full of advertisements and I answered one of these adverts, came down to Brighton one evening and met this chap with whom I'd corresponded.

JOHN: We also had a whole selection of gay novels, which we sold by mail order. Reading was quite a popular hobby at that time. And especially if there was a gay novel, everybody read it. We read everything that came out, avidly. There were three came out in America called, 'Song of the Loon', 'Song of Aaron' and 'Listen, the Loon Sings'. A gay trilogy. Those were the first really erotic gay books. I mean by the end of the first or second page you were almost having a spontaneous orgasm. Fantastic books. We re-established the copyright and we published the three of those here in Brighton. They were a spectacular success.

'Song of the Loon' — classic gay pornography of 1969.

Now people began to come to us with their problems because we were the only gay organisation. Although we didn't call ourselves a gay organisation in the sense of the Homosexual Law Reform Society. We were never set up as a gay charity. We were always a gay business. The money did come in and it came in very fast. And we were giving information on the telephone. We had, I guess, what was effectively the predecessor of Gay Switchboards. People had our phone number from the magazine. They used to ring up about gay places. And we seemed to be the custodian of gay information. We were giving people advice, people were writing to us. We even employed a full time secretary whose whole purpose was helping people who wrote in with their problems. People came to our office, just arriving on the doorstep, with their problems. It was quite dramatic. There was this boy from somewhere in the Lake District, just arrived. He ran away from home. His mother had been killed in a road accident, caused by his father. His sister had now got married and therefore he had nobody in the family to turn to and didn't see any point in staying there. He had no job, nowhere to live, nothing . . . Well, we helped him as best we could. Another guy read an article about us in the Evening Argus. And he paced up and down Preston Street for day after day, trying to get enough courage to come in. Finally he did come in and, well, he needed help to come out of the closet, as it were. A term which still hadn't been invented at that moment but anyway, he wanted to tell his family that he was gay and just didn't know how to go about it and how to pluck up the courage. We helped him.

♥   ♥   ♥

GERALD: I didn't have any trouble with the police personally, but, of course one has read about it over the years, particularly in the Argus, and in those days there were weekend papers called the Brighton and Hove Herald, and the Brighton and Hove Gazette. And these cases were very much publicised in the media, and friends that I know who did fall foul of prosecution, they were always much more nervous of the media than they were of the police. There was a fine, perhaps a hefty one, attached to it, whatever it was, importuning, or gross indecency or whatever the charge was, but the greatest worry to them was that they would lose their jobs if it was in the press. If it didn't appear in the press, they hoped that they would get away with it. But in those days almost everything of that nature — because, of course, reporters were much cheaper, the salaries and everything, and therefore they could have full coverage on all the courts, and very little escaped in that way — nearly everything like that was reported, because it was considered notorious conduct.

JAMES: Those were the terrible days when the law was very harsh on people particularly cottaging because it was in a way easier for people to take risks in cottages rather than live together and be known by the neighbours to be consenting criminals in private. More people did use to take risks. And I always remember poor old George from the Friese-Green, who got caught and fined something quite nasty, even in the fifties, something like £25, which was an awful lot of money but everybody would turn out, everybody that heard, to give support at the Court and then for some days afterwards the victim couldn't go into a pub or a club without being stood rounds by everybody. It was a sort of co-operative, a sympathy movement to all our fellow criminals.

GRANT: You had to be a little careful about picking people up in toilets. You had to be careful. You could make a mistake. Because the police at one time were very much of the idea that they could put some rather dishy policeman in and encourage you to do wrong and then have you up. They've always done it. We always used to say that's because they hadn't got anything in the book at the end of the week. They had to go and get something. And they go and pick a gay bloke up.

JAMES: Cottaging, of course, had almost an attraction to it. The risk element gave it a bit of a thrill, the risk of getting caught. There was very little mugging threat in those days, it was nearly all risks of policemen hiding in the broom cupboard and peering out through the grating in the top, things like that. And yet people used to be quite outrageous in their cottaging. Most people didn't do anything down there, they merely had a look to see what was being flashed at them and maybe picked someone up and took them home. There wasn't a lot actually went on, even in cubicles, to my knowledge. People were not totally reckless in what they did. There were always funny stories about it too, for people who'd never come to grief in it. I can remember Black Lion Street, opposite the Cricketers, there was a notorious downstairs gents there which has long since been closed by the police and somebody used to say they used to have to go down every day with a feather duster to dust the cobwebs off because people were down there all day and cobwebs were actually growing on them. Others would say that they go down with a packed lunch to spend the day there. That's the sort of lighthearted way that cottaging was regarded.

PETER: I believe the toilets at Debenhams — which wasn't Debenhams then, it was Plummer Roddis — when they had their restaurant, it was known you could meet people there, go for a morning coffee and find a bit of trade at the same time.

GEORGE: Let me explain. If you're sixteen or seventeen, you're aware of sex, and it's not the society you live in today, right? The society you live in today, you're more aware of sexuality, you're more aware of places you can go. When I was a kid, sixteen, seventeen, there were lots and lots of toilets around in Hove and Brighton. And I suspect, and I can't say this is true, but they were the places that people met.

STEVEN: One of my favourites was the Clock Tower, I always used to do very well there. There were the cop shop boxes round the corner, there was always the law hanging around. But some of the things I've seen down the Clock Tower's nobody's business. There were the three cubicles and if you got into the middle one, there was two holes in the wall. I was in the middle cubicle once and this young kiddy came in, couldn't have been more than fourteen, fifteen, and straight away took all his clothes off and he had a hard on and that. He pushed a note through the little hole, was I interested? Of course I was. He said, 'Where can we go?' I said, 'Well, I'll think of something.' So we met up top in front of the clock, and I was rattling my brains because I'd got to have him. The only place I could think of was the place I was staying up in Elm Grove, and I thought, with any luck the others will be at work. So we got a taxi back and went in, and touch wood, there was nobody in. We jumped into bed, we must have been there a good hour. We did everything, fucking, blow-job, and all the rest of it and it was very nice. He was way under age, even I was, I was only seventeen then. But somebody come in. Of course, I thought, 'How do I get him out?' Soon as they come in the door, what hard I did have just went straight down because I was panicking. If they found out a fourteen-year-old had been in the bedroom — all sorts of problems. But I did manage to get him out without them knowing and I did see him again. We managed to exchange phone numbers and we met a few times after that. We used to have to meet out in the country, safe somewhere, where there was nobody about. It was a bit awkward but we did manage to enjoy each other a few more times.

DENNIS: What killed the cottages was the 1960s when women got the Pill, and all of a sudden, women became available. Because they weren't available in those days; you were either married and you'd got a wife — in that case you were alright — or if you weren't married your girlfriend usually wouldn't let you do anything, so I think that's why all this activity went on in the cottages. We always called it trade and that's what it was. They weren't gay these people, they were just randy and wanted serving. And there were always people like me that were willing.

> 66 In a cottage, if there were lots of people there you felt safe. You were part of a brotherhood.
> ARTHUR 99

GRANT: Brighton was the humming place. First and foremost, there was the Men's Beach. There was so much beauty down there, I mean, you had to have binoculars to get it all in. It was too fantastic. Everybody knew about the Men's Beach. There was nothing in the rest of the country to compare. So of course, all these people that came down on holiday, they just went down, if the weather was fine, they probably slept there all night. Of course they never went in the sea, they never got their beautiful bikinis wet. Half of them would be, 'Oh, my God! No! I'm afraid of the water!' They'd be afraid of a great big limpet coming up and biting them.

If you went far enough down, there was no such thing as wearing any clothing, and it was quite a wide stretch of beach too. It was probably one whole space between two groynes. And on a weekend in the summer, you literally had to find a spot about a foot square. And you just walked around and when you found somebody that hadn't got a friend, or wasn't talking, you sat yourself down, and started chatting away. And if you didn't click, well, you got up and you walked around again. So it was a continuous circle of people walking around, and suddenly sitting, then upping and round again. It was quite amusing. It was men only. If there were any women or children strayed on it they were promptly told to get off. Lots of very famous and infamous people could have been photographed on the Men's Beach, I can assure you. The reason that it was shut after many, many years, I'm talking about probably twenty or thirty years, was because along there the police convalescent home had some police huts and the police came along one day and bulldozed the sign down. That was the end of the Men's Beach. They have never ever got anything quite like it in Brighton since. I mean the nudist beach, right up at the Marina, is nothing compared to that old Men's Beach.

PETER: I was a bit scared of the Men's Beach because it was notoriously gay. It was occasionally patrolled by the police. I kept away from it, because I was a bit worried about my professional reputation. Not only the Men's Beach at Hove, there was the Gas-works. Up here in Kemptown was another trolling-ground for them. Then there was another one at Peacehaven, a nude beach at Peacehaven. Been up there a couple of times, not to do anything, we used to sunbathe in the nude, you see, troll around and there was little caves and things, rocks where you could hide behind and have a bit of trade. But I never did anything like that, again because I was a bit scared.

♥   ♥   ♥

ERIC: My sex life started when I came to Brighton, when I was forty-six. I got a bed-sitter in Temple Street for 25 bob a week and a job on the West Pier selling ice-cream. I used to have a couple of purple hearts, with purple hearts you became less inhibited, and two pints of bitter and walk along the front and the first boy I liked the look of, I used to say, 'Would you like to come home with me?' And more often than not, they said, 'Yes.' They'd always want a pair of socks or shirt or breakfast the next morning and things like that. And they used to get ten bob, that was the thing people gave them.

100

Top left Dennis in 1957.
Above Eric, Brighton beach, 1951.
Left Palace Pier.

101

Eric outside seafront cottage.

66 I wasn't good at cottaging, I'm not very well hung. I was also a bit nervous about being caught. I did do it but I wasn't a regular cottager. A lot of people spent their lives doing it, didn't they?
ERIC 99

GERALD: Somebody once asked me how one gay person could tell another when they were walking along the street and they hadn't been introduced and it was purely a language of the eyes, you see it was a question of recognition, even if they continued going on, there was a knowledge that was conveyed, perhaps it was the fact that they didn't drop their eyes too quickly, which said, 'Hello.' Which formed that point of recognition. But it wasn't something you could teach anybody, it was something you acquired, as you grew up. When I was a very young teenager, I couldn't understand how people knew instinctively. And then, of course, it gradually comes upon one, as one gets a little older and more experienced, and meets more people. I'm not talking about the bars, I'm talking about outside of the bars, in the theatre, concert hall, just walking along the street, sitting on the beach, and so on. I don't know any other way to describe it. It certainly was purely the eyes. It's something you learnt or had to learn.

GRANT: You could tell the way they look at you. Usually tell from the eyes. Didn't always work but eyes usually gave it away. We always used to say blue eyes were more inclined to be homosexual than brown eyes. We used to call it bedroom eyes. It's an expression that I can't really explain. Some people have got it and some haven't.

DAVID: I used to pick up men in the street and in pubs and all that. I was a bit of a tart, basically. It wasn't only in gay pubs, I hardly ever did go with a man who was gay, mostly it was men who were kind of on the loose. I did prefer masculine men and so I was mostly passive.

And down Trafalgar Street there used to be all these houses that were abandoned and neglected and you used to take men there, into these houses, and have sex in those empty rooms.

JAMES: Generally the person being followed would know and would encourage and would stop to look in a window, and the other person would come up and say, 'That's nice, isn't it?' You'd say, 'Oh, yes. Well, I've got one like that at home, d'you fancy seeing it?' That sort of thing. And there was an awful lot of the cigarette thing, you know: 'Have you got a light?' There was the dreadful case of someone who literally wanted to light a cigarette and went up to an airman in Queens Road and said, 'Excuse me, have you got a light?' and the airman looked straight ahead of him, and said, 'I only fuck women.'

♥   ♥   ♥

GRANT: The queans used to go up to the station. That was the last thing they'd all do because on a Saturday night a lot of the sailors didn't have a weekend pass, they had to go back. There was a last train from Brighton to Portsmouth and it left just about half past one. And those sailors, who had been drinking literally all day, would make their way up Queens Road to the station and wait for the last train to go to Portsmouth. That was

> ❝ I met Godfrey Winn one night in the Black Lion Street cottage and he took me off in his Rolls Royce somewhere. We tried to have trade but he was absolutely useless.
> PETER ❞

where the queans in drag used to descend like a plague of locusts! They'd all go up in taxis and you could see them, rushing through the station, in high heeled shoes, covered in sequins, with wigs, made up with eyelashes two inches long, with trains, so pissed that they were falling arse over tip to find a sailor. Of course, the cottage at the station used to be infamous. They used to climb up and take the lights out of the cubicles so it was dark and all go in with torches so they could see exactly where they were. That was quite something.

ERIC: I have had some very nasty experiences. I picked up one guy who was absolutely hopeless in bed. He was very uncouth, he was belching and farting and very bad mannered. And in the morning he had a flick knife and he started throwing it against the door and I wasn't very happy, so I said, 'Come on, let's go out and have breakfast at Lyon's,' there used to be a Lyon's tea shop and I managed to get him out of the house. But two days after that, a lorry driver was murdered and this boy answered the description.

Another time there was a boy I knew called Peter, who was rent, he used to come and see me every weekend for a Sunday matinee, he stopped me with a friend of his by the Labour Exchange and pushed me into a doorway. This was broad daylight. He made out he had a razor in his pocket and he said, 'Look, if you don't give me money, I'm going to slash you.' Luckily I was quite strong then and I pushed him away. I told him he wouldn't get a farthing from me and they both ran off.

GRANT: Thurlow Arms, Edward Street, it's not so very far from the old Brighton market, and a lot of the barrow boys went in there. They are very attractive to a certain type of people, they are to me 'cause I love their humour. They were wide boys but there was something very earthy, down to earth with them, they were very attractive. They were cheeky, didn't stand on ceremony at all. You could be sitting in the Thurlow Arms, quietly having a drink, and two or three of them would come in, and one would just come up to you straight away and say, 'Cor, yor bloody alright, I fancy you. Having a drink?' You'd say, 'Yes, thank you very much.' And they'd join you, and before you knew where you were, he was rubbing your leg, and if you fancied him you'd say, 'Shall we call a taxi?' He would say, 'Well, that's what I'm here for.' He was probably married. But they were very attractive.

JOHN: There's a very old English saying, 'Needs must when the Devil drives'. If you have to pay rent for a bed sitting room and you haven't a job and your benefit is less than the rent and you don't want to be homeless, you have to make it up from somewhere. And since I didn't see anything wrong, although a lot of people did and perhaps still do in this strange land, I didn't see anything wrong with cashing in on one's assets. I'm perhaps lucky that nature endowed me in a rather spectacular way and people used to say if I sold it by the inch I'd have been a millionaire. I was very successful. I didn't go to pick up men, they picked me up, and so I would say to them, 'Well, I think you're very attractive, and yes I'd like to have sex with you, but unfortunately at this time of my life I have to make a business of it.' And then they'd say, 'Well, how much do you charge?' And I say, 'Well I don't, I'll leave it to your generosity. Because I have a need and you have a need and

Thurlow Arms.

104

we can help each other and enjoy doing it.' And when you do it like that of course it's not so much selling it as accepting gifts from grateful admirers. I mean the net result is the same, except that you do make more money that way than if you say, 'Well, this is my price.' Or even if you set it out as a menu in a restaurant. Sometimes I wouldn't get money but I would be taken out for a rather nice dinner which is equally acceptable. Or bought clothes, all kinds of possibilities you know. But hard cash in my hand was the usual way and it was quite acceptable at the time.

There was always this taboo about it, it was a deterrent, you did it if you really had to. And then there was Adrian who had what you might call a sugar-daddy in Ardingly. And there were other people with wealthy supporters. But that's also prostitution, but with one customer rather than a lot of different customers. And well, it was fun.

I was taken out on the cliff by somebody in a car one day and he had some fetish that he wanted me to get out of the car and drop my pants and masturbate or do something or other. I had to do it outside the car while he sat in the car watching, and of course I got out of the car and started doing whatever he had asked me to do and he drove off at high speed and left me there. Oh, I had some very odd people came, strange people.

There were a lot of people who were just lonely, they didn't particularly want sex, they just wanted someone to be with, talk to, tell their problems to, or something like that. Just wanted someone to go out to dinner and have a drink or have a chat. There were plenty of people like that. So it wasn't always just for hard-nosed sex, for many it was often just a social thing.

JAMES: I think the sort of rent here locally tended to be straight young men, who knew how to make a few bob without getting themselves into trouble. The one thing they would never allow would be for anyone to poke them, therefore they didn't run any medical risk. If they could get ten shillings for a wank, well, they were quite happy, thank you very much, and then they'd take the girlfriend out to the pictures with it. That was the sort of rough boy who'd learned the source of money. They were around, and maybe a member might bring one into a club and, if they were not openly accosting people for money but just behaving in a friendly manner, it's nobody's business what happens afterwards. They weren't known to be threatening or exploiting anybody, but they certainly weren't what we would call gay themselves, they would just be worldly wise lads who knew how to make a few bob.

EDDIE: I didn't earn a lot of money and if somebody came to me and said, 'I'll give you a fiver to go to bed,' I had no illusions about compromising myself. Five pound was five pound and wasn't to be sneezed at. I only earned about three, four pound a week, so five pound was a lot of money. And that mainly paid for my clothes because I was a lot dressier in those days. I wore things like white suits, and that was all the rage.

Brighton was buzzing in those days. If you didn't want to work, you didn't have to work. I had a period where I didn't work, I suppose six months. I could go in, in the morning, to Chatfield's, have a sing-song, didn't cost me. It probably did but I can't remember. I seemed to be eternally with money in my hand. I was never short of money.

> 66 Quite often I think it's got to be the bloody-minded people, the people who don't mind being the heretics, particularly in those days when we were actually illegal. We weren't just unconventional, we were illegal, dangerous criminals, we could be put away for life. I think it was often as much a matter of independence of thought and independence of personality that encouraged people to be gay.
> JAMES 99

I remember once, I was with a girl and a famous actor came into Chatfield's and he sent a boy over and he said, 'I'll give you £100.' I was with a girl at the time so that was a non-starter. You met all sorts, you met some strange people. Then there was the guy that had the restaurant at the Clock Tower. He was a strange man. I didn't know him by name but everybody knew him. He used to go to bed with his boys and he liked eating cream cakes. He did! He was kinky! And he was a great big rotund man, he was a huge man! And then there was Gerry Buxton. He had access to a lot of speed tablets and he used to get his boys and give them speed and get them to bed. These were well known people.

JAMES: Near the Grand Hotel there were a row of grotty little cafes, frequented by all sorts. A local woman councillor got an obsession about late night coffee bars and what evil places they are and how teenagers were being led into all sorts of wickedness and so much so that eventually she got a Bill through Parliament. I think anything staying open after midnight had to get a licence from the police or from the Justices or something of that sort. But that was a Brighton-based thing. There was no such demand anywhere else in the country but I think a national law was made as a result of the ravings of this local lady.

GRANT: There was also a cafe on the front, very near where the Brighton Centre is now. It was so low that you wouldn't be seen dead in it, but it was open all night and all the rent boys used to go in there for late coffee and just sit there until someone came in and — clicked. But there were quite a number of coffee bars like that. The coffee was diabolical, you never drank it, you just bought it and left it.

JAMES: One of these tatty little cafes on the lower prom was called The Wanderin and it was presided over by a very wealthy, large, fat man, quite six feet tall and enormously fat who'd obviously come from quite a good family background He just loved being on his knees in front of young men, particularly if they were in uniform. George, his name was, always known as Fat Emma and he ran this sleazy Wanderin. And if we went in there we wouldn't have tea or coffee because you wouldn't trust the washing up. You'd have a bottle of coke with a straw because that was the only safe thing to drink. And he was quite outrageous with his picking up of soldiers and things. It was always said of poor Emma that he choked to death on a guardsman's chopper!

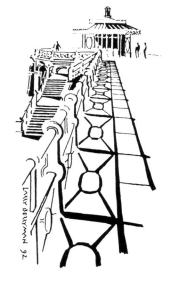

Seafront promenade and railings.

PETER: In those days before KY it was always Vaseline, used to make a hell of a mess with the bedclothes, there was always Vaseline and a bit of spit. If you couldn't get Vaseline there was a bit of haircream, bit of Brylcreem. I remember going in a restaurant with a friend and a rather camp waitress thought we were a couple. The friend happened to ask for some more butter, because your butter portions in a restaurant were very meagre indeed and the waitress said, 'Yes, dear, what are you doing with it, using it for immoral purposes?' But as I said, where there's a will there's a way, if you can't buy any grease use a bit of spit to get the juices going, a bit of spit does just as well.

'Is he butch or bitch?' they used to say. If you were bitch, you buried your head in the pillow and if you were butch you got on top. It was active or passive you see. You very rarely came across those words on the gay scene. It was either is she butch or bitch. Though the camp one could sometimes be the very active one — if she was a butch fairy.

BUCK: Everybody was known. You were either feminine or masculine. In those days one did know who was Arthur and who was Martha but today, you really don't know. Often you would meet a person in a club and then a friend would come up and say, 'Oh, it's no good playing about with her, you know, she's a raving quean.'

GRANT: There was an expression that he was 'Rosy Bothways'. That meant that, according to his partner, he would be amenable. The word is bisexual which sounds so pretty now. Everybody got labelled and we would always discuss it. 'Oh, well, those two are together and he's he and she's she. Now why was she out with her? She should have been out with him and she wasn't.' If you fancied someone, the word would go round the bar and somebody would find out for you which they were. But it was best to be 'Rosy Bothways' so's you never got disappointed.

JAMES: People tended to have an image of themselves as butch or bitch, this was as much a matter of prestige as anything. They were very worried about their image. It was always assumed that fucking was the main sexual activity but I had the impression that mutual wanking was the most common activity. There were other things we didn't know a lot about in those days. Even among the fraternity, variations of interest like S&M or leather were kept very, very hush-hush and nobody knew except those who were intimately involved. There was the story of the gentleman who was well into water sports which struck us as a most odd exercise. There was a sort of orthodoxy within people's own minds.

GRANT: In the fifties you still had to be slightly careful of disease, but you didn't have AIDS. I mean, I don't know what people do now, they can't throw discretion to the winds quite as much as we did. We were far more flagrant, I think, than people are now. You didn't really think twice in the fifties. You had to be careful to a point, yes, but, if you caught any of the diseases in the fifties you didn't die. With a couple of shots of penicillin, oil of penicillin, you were alright within about three months.

JAMES: One of the strange things, when we think of AIDS, was how lightly people took VD in those days. Some of the screaming queans would be quite brazen about their visits to the special clinic and it was all a big laugh and yet at the same time, I've seen barmen in the bars, if they've had the least suspicion about someone who'd just gone out, I've seen them break the glass and throw it away. Quite unnecessary.

Drag night at the 42 Club

GRANT: Queans in Brighton were so bold. I mean they would go into a mixed pub — the Spotted Dog in particular where it was mostly normal in front and queer at the back — I've known them go straight up to somebody in the front bar and say, 'Oh, I fancy you, darling, you've got the most lovely eyes, can I buy you a drink?' They were very brazen to the extent that if somebody had said, 'Piss off, you silly old quean,' they'd say, 'Oh, get you, Ada!' And try somebody else within a couple of yards. I've seen it so often. Go straight up, without the slightest demur and say, 'You're lovely, can I buy you a drink? What are you drinking, dear? Ooh! Don't drink beer when I'm here! Let me open my purse. What are you doing tonight? Oh, not on your own! You're not on your own any more.'

PETER: There were some camp people about, I know two or three used to terrify me to death. They used to camp themselves gutless on the seafront at night. I used to have to run up a side street to get out of their way because they knew I was one of the boys. They just flaunted it completely, very, very camp. They were disliked for it, people said, 'Oh, keep away from those awful people.' But there was nothing awful about them, they were just outrageously camp, they'd scream across the road, 'Hello, darling.' Well, in those days you just didn't do that sort of thing.

GRANT: If you passed a building site, most of the builders would whistle after you, call out after you, or pretend to walk like they thought you were walking, in other words mincing about. If you were bold, you would go back and you would retaliate. Some could do it, some didn't want to do it, some didn't want to make a fuss, others were too shy. You could belittle them if you had a vitriolic tongue, like a lot of them had, you could send them up so that they didn't know which way of the week they were. Words can kill. If you know the right ones to use at the right time. You can be very objectionable with words. So they sometimes bit off more than they could chew. You could also get whistled at in the fifties by taxi drivers, bus drivers, lorry drivers, especially long distance, great, big, buck lorry drivers, they leaned out and leered out of their cab and said something. I did once turn round and say, 'Piss off, you silly quean, I expect you turn over anyway!' He was rather shocked, he nearly drove into another lorry but there you are. You had to be prepared and you probably thought up something rather belligerent or brilliant before you went out. We used to do that. A lot. We had wicked tongues. We used to think up some very good lines. Oh, no, we were never caught short.

PETER: Millie had a very wicked tongue. She flounced in there one day, into the Variety Club, for a quick scotch. She stopped dead in her tracks and looked at us all sitting in the window and said, 'Oh God! Who arranged you lot? Moisy Stevens?' Moisy Stevens, the famous florist who was actually the florist to the Queen Mum. 'Who arranged you lot?' she says, 'Moisy Stevens?' At which we all shrivelled.

GEORGE: I was in the Greyhound one night, upstairs and some naffs came up, as we called them, and started going, 'Hey, hey up, poofs!' and all this kind of nonsense and there was a bit of embarrassment, they were thrown out. Well, later on that night we were in Chatfield's and they were in there with three girls. And these queans walked in and said, 'Hello, sweets, you weren't like that just now, were you, when you were in the gay bar with us!' Well, there was such an altercation between these blokes and their women, explaining what they were doing in gay bars and these queans coming up to them, I mean it was divine retribution. Wonderful stuff, wonderful stuff. I remember, another time, one quean was in some sort of rough house trouble and he dropped his voice and goes, 'I'll beat you fucking lot up, you pick on me!' And when they went away, he went, 'Oh, thank gawd for that, dear. My 'eart can't stop beating.' It was all front. We had this front thing going.

GRANT: If we got sent up by a shop assistant, they were marooned behind the counter. That was what was so nice ! They couldn't move away. They couldn't walk away. They had to listen. They had to hear it. You never sent a queer up if you were behind the counter in a shop because you got the full volume, 'Who is this little counter jumper? Dear! Dear! Dear! I wonder if the manager knows that we won't be using this shop again? And taking all our friends away? I wonder if he realises how much custom he's lost? What an impertinent little prick!' Well, after about another ten minutes of that he didn't usually send a queer up again. We could be very wicked.

♥   ♥   ♥

DENNIS: You have to vada the camp Polari if you want to know what you're doing. That was something, also that was pre the 1967 Act. It was a secret way of talking to one another. It's based on Italian. Like 'vada' means look, you see. 'Bona' means good. And 'cartso' is an Italian word for cock or prick. You had to be very careful when you were using the camp Polari in Italy because Italians understood it. I was out with Percy, we were in Rimini and we were walking down the street and this lovely man coming towards us and she says, 'Oh, vada the cartso on that' and he hit her straight in the eye. Bang! She said, 'What was all that about?' I said, 'Well, you did say, "Vada his Cartso", dear.' You forget these fucking Italians know what it means! So a man's an 'omi', a female's a 'palone'. The only thing that wasn't Italian was 'riah' for hair and that's 'hair' spelt backwards. I was never very good at it myself, but I knew a lot of queans what were!

TED: If anybody wore a hairpiece it was, 'Mm, nanty riahs, dear.' If it was particularly bad, in those days, the Brighton expression was, 'Riah by Fludes' - Fludes being a carpet shop.

> **"** Rex Holland, like a lot of queans then, had a very quick way with words. I remember Rose Filk'n had got an exceedingly expensive watch, worth thousands and thousands. Ray said to her, 'Oh, you know you really shouldn't wear that out. I mean they'd cut your wrists off to get that!' And Rex quietly said, 'Wear it round your throat, dear. . .' JAMES **"**

GEORGE: You just said something, 'Vada that dish over there' or 'Vada that cruet' or 'vada those lallies'. You know, nobody knew what the hell you were talking about. 'Vada those lallies', look at those legs, you know. So if somebody sat next to you, they wouldn't know, would they? If I said to some man who walked in, 'Oh, vada those lallies', they'd think nothing about it but, 'Look at those legs', they'd think, 'My god, what have we got next to us.' So that's the sort of time you used it. But then it was also a camp, 'Oh, get her lallies, dear!'

HARRY: Everybody had nicknames in those days. You never used their ordinary names. You know, sometimes you wondered who they were talking about if they used their ordinary name.

GRANT: There were so many nicknames: Foxtrot Phyllis, Dame Myra Hess, Lady Precious Stream, Petshop Nell, Deaf Ada, Miss Mattress, Tatty Tony, Cider Lil. Two, an affair — two that always used to be together, were the same height, looked rather similar, they looked like two peas in a pod — they were called the Bookends. Some nicknames were funny, some were rude, some were very unkind.

HARRY: When I first met Bob, I was rather staid and was used to wearing suits, formal suits, and collars and ties and things like that. In those days, casual wear hadn't really sort of taken off. And Bob used to have a habit of picking very nice things and I used to say, 'Oh, I like that, I think I'll have one of those,' so we weren't identically dressed but somebody once, it was Bettie Harrod, she was a very nice lady that was very famous in Brighton with the gays, she used to love them and she said one day 'Oh my God,' she said, 'you look like a couple of bookends,' and of course, the name stuck and we were never referred to as anything else except the Bookends!

BOB: There's not many people know us as the Bookends now.

HARRY: Not now but I mean, in those days, when we were a member of the society, as you might say, everybody knew us, they'd say, 'The Bookends.' And then of course, there was famous Aunt Rose, little dapper man, he was, and he lived with his affair, Esme, who was the taller one. They were both couturiers really, they'd both been trained in Paris and Aunt Rose had been trained by Worth. And they had the first gay casual clothes shop here in Brighton in Bond Street.

BOB: They did all the gay clothes, gay casuals for the gay people here. And Brighton really revolved round Aunt Rose and Aunt Esme because they were the inner sanctum and if you were on their list, well, you were in. They used to have tea parties every Sunday afternoon and if you were invited to the tea party, you were in!

HARRY: You were in Burke's Peerage more or less.

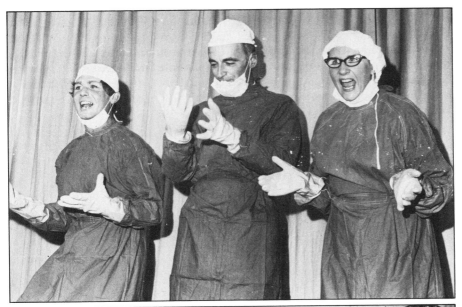

'It was roaring.'
Top Tommy Kent, Tony Stuart and Joyce Golding in a sketch from Brighton Gayest, 1969.
Left and bottom Drag nights at the 42 Club.

BOB: Aunt Rose used to sit at a high chair and pour tea out of silver tea pots.

HARRY: In her Queen Anne chair she used to sit and play and everybody used to go and greet her. She used to sit there, like the Duchess, pouring out the tea. There'd be sometimes as many as forty people. You knew everybody. It was rather like a masons' lot, I suppose. They had a beautiful flat in Albert Mansions in Hove.

BOB: Sandy Wilson composed 'The Boyfriend' in their flat.

♥ ♥ ♥

PETER: There was a lot of interesting characters about in those days. There was a so-called baron, a Baron Nugent that used to live in Wick Hall, I think he was a self-styled Irish baron, he was always known as the Baron Nugent from the Wicked Hall. I understand the story goes he used to take little chickens back and he used to make them keep changing their swim shorts. There was a tall, very thin quean, rather camp, quite well known in the clubs in those days, and I'm going back to the 42 Club days and the Curtain Club days, he was tall, very skinny, he was known as Languid Lil. Then there was another very camp quean, who used to use the club circuit in those days, youngish fellow, quite good looking, extremely camp, limp wristed, minced everywhere, known as Betty Lou.

GRANT: Count William de Belleroche was almost an alcoholic. And he would think nothing of spending a lot of money and when I'm saying a lot, £10 in those days was a fortune, when you're thinking of 3/6d for a whisky, if you spent £10, you can imagine, it was a fortune. He had a chauffeur and a butler and he had an old Rolls — I think he must have bought it from Queen Mary because you didn't have to bow your head to get in it, you opened the door and you walked straight in! And he used to sit in the back, it was a cabriolet, the front part was open and it was only the back part that was covered in. He had a bête noire, his bête noire was Baron Nugent. And they were like sodium and water, they were always fighting, verbally and also fisticuffs if needs be. They were both alcoholics. If somebody that neither of them liked joined them, they would suddenly become buddies and friends. Both of them had the wickedest tongues you could ever imagine. They were vitriolic and vile. They all used to try and be so wicked, they thought it was amusing. And smart. And attractive. And actually, it was not always, it was rather childish.

DAVID: In the late sixties, William de Belleroche picked me up on Brighton station. The first thing he said to me was, 'Are you on the run from the police?' He used to totter round Brighton picking up rough trade at night, all sorts of people and take them to his house on Black Rock and give us all food and drink. And he was very patronising, rather offensively patronising as I come to remember it. He took a shine to me and I was his favourite for about three weeks. I used to go there in the daytime and clean his car, which he used to pay me for. I can't remember what it was that made me fall out of favour but I mean, I didn't last all that long. Nobody ever did.

He wasn't sexually involved with anybody, he was a voyeur. He was fifty-seven at the time, a bit worn out, rather world weary, rather bitter. And when he died, he left everything that he owned, which was quite a lot, to his secretary and companion. I don't think his family were best pleased about that.

EDDIE: Count William de Belleroche suffered with insomnia, so he stayed awake all night and he'd invite you up there for dinner and that could be at three o'clock in the morning and there was always a weird collection of people. There was Sir Francis Rose, he was a strange guy, a painter. There was a guy called Lord Churchill, who was supposed to be related to Winston Churchill. There was Countess Paula, another relative of his. Or the Chief of Police, he'd have the Chief of Police to dinner. He had six siamese cats. He'd never pay you money but he had a big roulette wheel and he would give you money by letting you win at roulette. But he was a strange character. He was a good painter. He painted fish that looked like people.

KAY: All of the taxi drivers knew Willie the Count. He was a count, actually. I thought, 'It's no good trying to impress me because my mother was surrounded by counts in her life, two a penny, find them in any Casino or Kursaal. Pick them up as you pick up pins.' He played with people. He didn't play with me because we understood each other very well indeed. I think he knew by my manner: 'I'm not condemning your set-up, you live as you like, as far as I'm concerned. But don't expect me to play games or be taken in.' Very good looking man, very charming and when he talked about artists, he was very interesting indeed.

BUCK: Dame Myra was a character, one of the old school. Never went out without her tiara. He really was a wonderful pianist, he could play anything. And he'd have the whole top of the piano lined with gins. He'd play at the clubs in London and a lot of the gay clubs here. And he was very well known. They'd suddenly announce, 'We now have Dame Myra Hess to play for us!' And then he'd get up on the piano there. But everybody had to shut up, otherwise you'd hear a terrific bang as he slammed the top of the piano down.

JAMES: Betty Lou was quite a well known drag artist in clubs in Brighton and London. She'd been touring with the show, 'Belle of New York' which had a Salvation Army theme. It was at the Hippodrome. And up in Powis Square, which was quite a gay community in those days, there was somebody in a flat was going to give a party and some of the cast from this show were invited after the Saturday night last performance. And I can always remember, there was a basement area to this flat and Dolly, the famous Dolly, pianist from the Spotted Dog, was there and they'd wheeled a little upright piano out into the area and she was playing away merrily. It was probably midnight or later and the square was all in darkness and in the distance the sound of a big bass drum was heard, BOOM, BOOM, BOOM, BOOM and around the square came this outrageous character, Bettie Lou, dressed in Salvation Army ladies 1890s-style frock, the skirts

66 What was so extraordinary in the Terrace, I'd take Sunny out first thing on the dogs' lawn in what I call my morning slacks and sweater, having just brushed my teeth and pushed my hair back and the rest of us were like that, rather. There was Dougie Byng, my dear, all dressed up to the nines, waistcoat, everything - terribly elegant in a sort of twenties, thirties way - with his little shopping basket, putting us all to shame. KAY 99

to the ankle, leading the Salvation army band from the show and doing high kicks with her tambourine, kicking the tambourine at shoulder height as she came round the square to join in this party. I can remember the lights going on, like in a Disney film, around the square.

HARRY: Oh, Betty Lou was a very famous character, I think she's still alive, but I think she's a recluse now. But she was quite outrageous, she was very theatrical, she was a proper theatre person and she used to get in films. We all went to the pictures to look for Betty Lou! She was in 'Oh, What a Lovely War!' as a soldier. She used to do miming things. She was very good at it actually. She used to get in her drag and her mouth moves were quite perfect. I always remember, one of the best ones she did which I liked very much, she did a real spoof number on 'The Jewel Song' from Gounod's Faust. She'd sit there and do the little soulful bit, then she'd sing, 'I must be gay' and she'd got hundreds and hundreds of necklaces and bracelets — she was shoving them all on! She was like a Christmas tree when she'd finished! But her mouth moves never, never left the words at all. She was very clever and she used to give marvellous parties but they were always fancy dress, hers. You always had to go dressed up to Betty Lou's parties. They all had a theme, we had a Tramp Party at Betty Lou's. Then we went once to Petshop Nell's party dressed up as two chocolate soldiers. It was a Twenties Party. We went as guardsmen because we had to be Bookends, you see. And of course all the queans went in their flappers things. And we were never short of partners all night — 'Oh, I must have a dance with the guardsman!' And then Cyril's was an Elegance Party. I went in an evening suit and a coronet and white gloves! Peer's coronet!

♥   ♥   ♥

SHEILA: In those days we had a lot of private parties. You know, probably when you went to the loo in the club, you'd bump into somebody and say, 'If you'd like to bring a bottle and come back, we're having a party.' I think there were more private parties. And they were quite good fun, because we'd do a bit of smoochy dancing and then we used to play spinning the bottle, that was the best part. Because if it went to someone who you'd had your eye on all evening and you went outside, you might be lucky to get into a clinch. Quite often you'd go on or maybe you'd get an invite for another evening, a weekend probably, to go to someone's home. There weren't that many places to go to so I think the tendency was that you went to private parties. Quite a few people would go but it would all be women.

SANDIE: There were a lot more parties in those days than there are now. There were masses of parties and we used to play party games too, like spin the bottle and all that rubbish but it was fun. We used to play murder and sardines and all those sort of screaming games, where everyone has an hysterical time and although they're kids' games, you really enjoyed it. You got around to kiss the person that you wanted to kiss that you would never normally get the opportunity to. We needed party games as our excuse to have a cuddle or a kiss with somebody other than our own partner.

VICKY: Oh, they were wonderful. Wonderful parties. There was a drink around at the time called Thunderbird and it was American wine with a kick like a mule. It really didn't taste terribly good but if you got the first drink down you you forgot about it. One drink and the taste didn't matter. And we used to have some all night parties, absolutely wonderful! And we'd end up all flaked out on settees and chairs and the floor and everywhere.

'Wonderful parties . . .'

GEORGE: I'd never been to a gay party. I'd been to gay clubs, I'd never been to an all gay party with lesbians and gay men, never. So, I forget where it was, somewhere like Fourth Avenue in Hove, or First Avenue, I don't know, one of those big things in the basement, and we went there, and there were sailors dancing with men which I found quite revolting. There were drag queans, Languid Lil looking in the mirror, I'd never seen a drag quean, just sit there looking at herself in the mirror all night. Steve was staying with me that night and this sailor came and asked him to dance. I was really incensed about this, I mean dancing together. I got Steve and I kicked his arse from Fourth Avenue, Hove to Seven Dials, Buckingham Road, all the way. I kicked, shouted and bawled at him all the way, I was so angry. I was so angry. I suppose it must have been jealousy.

JOHN: Let's say that it was unusual for seven days to go by without an invitation to a party somewhere. There was a very lovable character called Betty Lou, who operated from the 42 Club, that was his drinking place. And he used to do drag shows and he was well known to all local gay people. He used to organise parties. Extravaganzas. And the way it worked was this: on Saturday night, you go out and have an early dinner, you go on to a club and as the evening progressed the word would be passed around where the party was that night; and the word came around that you needed a car and you should go to the end of the lower promenade, where incognito men would hand you a sealed envelope with instructions. And we set off, following these instructions, going off along the coast, and we got to Newhaven. The third milestone you start to look for a gate with a private path, a dirt track, and you followed that, and there was two paths crossing and this and that and the other, all complicated instructions. You had to follow them really literally, to the letter. And finally you ended up at some kind of a bunker. On the cliff near Newhaven. It was something to do with the last war. And it was derelict and deserted. And there were this series of concrete buildings. And we arrived there, but nobody knew who was organising this. Of course, we were not surprised to find Betty Lou in full flight. And he or she, depending on which way you look at it, collected plastic ice-cream cups. I mean in those days you couldn't go out to Woolworths and buy a packet of plastic cups so he'd been collecting these tubs for years. And you came and you were handed a plastic bag containing the buffet which was a sausage roll, a sandwich and God knows what, and the plastic ice-cream cup. And there was some sort of music rigged up and everybody was dancing. Because dancing between people of the same sex was more or less not allowed in the clubs at that time. Some places did allow it but were thought to be taking a risk. In those days it wasn't disco type dancing, I mean it was arms round slow smoochy and old fashioned dancing. Which was very sexy of course. And this went on the whole night long.

GERALD: There were people who used to give enormous parties in their houses, drinks parties. There was the theatre clique, not just the big names, but masses of people who had Equity cards. There was the leather clique — the motorbike crowd, there were several. And if one is a member of a particular bunch of people, one tends to develop friendships within that particular circle. When one goes out and about, one always consults with the circle as to whether there was anything on that night, and so on and so on. It just evolved perfectly naturally, like the stars.

HARRY: When we got our new house we wouldn't have parties because we'd seen so much muck made. I shall always remember a party at Petshop Nell's, somebody broke the Knole settee. So we said we're not having them come round our new house with us scratching our fingers to the bone to furnish it, for them to go and burn it with cigarettes. So we didn't. What we did, we had about four people at a time for a dinner party and had a proper civilised one.

JANICE: I did have one romantic experience in Brighton but I really would rather not mention that one. It was with quite a famous person who was in the charts at that time, who I met at a party in Hove, 'cause quite often there were parties, which you'd end up meeting someone at one of these clubs and they'd say, 'Party at so and so' and you didn't necessarily know who the people were even, you'd just simply grab a bottle and gatecrash, that was quite a popular thing in the sixties, not so much now, certainly was then. So we ended up in this beautiful penthouse flat in Hove and there I met this lady who I had a very brief liaison with for about three months or something but I'm not going to say anything about it, it's not really fair because they are still performing today and it wouldn't do. I didn't actually meet anybody else in Brighton because we were with our own crowd, you see.

VALERIE: I don't know how they got hold of it but I remember at one party we had an absolute laugh because we knew that Vi and Jackie had one of these things, I don't know what they're called, artificial whatnots, you know. What they did with it or whether they actually ever used it I have no idea but it made us laugh for a start that it was kept in a jewel box on a bedside cabinet, all locked up. And then one night we egged them on to show it to us. And when they took it out, it was black and so that caused another laugh of course.

JANICE: We all jumped off the end of the pier I remember once, as a dare, on New Year's Eve. It was horrendous, reported, I believe, in the Evening Argus at the time. My mother was furious yet again, all these dykes picked up on Brighton beach by the coastguard. I lost a shoe, I was most upset about that. I remember I had a false hairpiece, they were quite fashionable at the time, big sort of tall hairdos, and it came off in the sea, with my shoe, which is probably on a Parisian beach by now or wherever the other side of Brighton Channel is. I don't know, mad as hatters. It was freezing too, it was snowing I believe, bloody freezing. We just all did it for a dare, about six or seven of us. The ambulance came and we were all taken off to some hospital there to see if any of us had suffered a heart attack. Sobered us up, we could have killed ourselves, I mean it was just outrageous. Anyway they released us, they thought we'd probably be alright but we'd got nowhere to go, had we, we hadn't got any money, of course we'd spent it all, and we'd still got a lot of alcohol in us, anyway we were dragged off to the police station and spent the night in cells, where I might say, the WPC's at the time plied us with even more booze, telling us it would warm us up. It was New Year of course. I'm sure they knew we were gay, and I'm sure they were too, definitely, yes. Oh, it was fun, just jumped off the end of the pier, fortunately the tide was up.

❤   ❤   ❤

GEORGE: The 42 Club did gay shows at the Co-op hall in London Road. They did it for charity, for St John's Ambulance or something like that. A drag show and a gay show. They were revues. It was predominantly drag but there was wonderful stuff in it and really very funny. It's got to have been 'sixty-seven onwards. They had 'Brighton Gay', 'Brighton Gayer', 'Brighton Gayest'. There was a wonderful opening number, with everyone dressed as the Roman Legion, 'Tramp, tramp, tramp, the boys are out to camp,' and wonderfully witty numbers. There was another number, a lot of lesbians came on in tweeds and pork-pie hats, which was the identification of a lesbian then, singing 'Put your finger in the dyke.' Oh, wonderful stuff and very funny. They were very clever. They became quite popular and quite famous people came. I believe Diana Dors came down to see it one year.

PETER: They were an absolute riot. A total sell-out every year. They used to queue for tickets. Joyce Golding would always do her cod opera act. I remember they did a very funny number all dressed in leather gear and crash helmets singing, 'It'll be a butch night tonight.'

BOB: A quean we called the Milk Lady - he did a milk round - did a wonderful impersonation of Bette Davis. He was very good at Bette Davis. I remember a little song parody they did of three spinsters, looking over the cliffs at Telscombe at all the nudists there. They were very good shows. It was also very popular with straight people who were sympathetic to the gay people.

HARRY: They were always very well-rehearsed and very well-dressed. It was very witty, it wasn't all toffee-nosed. It used to be packed. It was one of the highlights of the season, was the 42 Club show.

SANDIE: One of the boys did a marvellous number - it's the one thing I shall always remember from those shows. He was very pretty, the other boys hated him, bitched him something rotten. He walked across the stage, empty stage, dressed as the Queen, in a grand frock with the most enormous train. He stopped mid-stage and looked at us all, an enigmatic smile on his face and we all tittered, wondering what on earth he was doing. Then he

The Forty Two Club presents
in aid of the British Red Cross Society   **PROGRAMME**

brighton gay
an intimate revue

brighton gay-er
the forty two club presents

brighton gay-est

PROGRAMME

disappeared off the stage. And this train kept going and going and the audience kept watching in silence. And then he reappeared at the end of the train, holding it, dressed as a page. I'd never seen that done before, it was absolutely fantastic, I fell about.

AILEEN: We used to see some of the shows that went on at the Co-op. Oh, they were wonderful, they were absolutely, absolutely superb. Absolutely out of this world. Whoever thought it up, their imagination was great. We never, ever missed that. When they came around every year, we always went. And you used to see the queue of all the gays, standing outside waiting to get in. And I said, 'If anyone came along in the bus, they'd say, 'Oh, look at all the gays there, look at them all.' And I'd say, 'Well, there you are. Point the finger now!' But oh, they were superb, those shows. That's all gone.

Biographies

Aileen was born in 1938 in Glasgow. Resident of Hove in the sixties. Worked in shop and office managerial positions. Now breadwinner for Harriet and the 'family'.

Annie Allen was born in 1919 in Northampton. Visitor to Brighton and resident of a village near Eastbourne in the fifties and sixties. Worked from home for the Daily Mail, answering letters to their Agony Aunt column and in the Probation service. Now enjoying a quiet life as a painter.

Arthur was born in 1923 in New Zealand. 'I've worked as a teacher for most of my life. Frequent visitor to Brighton. I now live very happily in Bath with my partner of 46 years standing.'

Barbara Bell was born in 1913 in Blackburn. ' I was resident in Brighton in the fifties and sixties and did teaching and approved school work. I now feel it a privilege and a delight to be included and accepted in Lesbian Line social activities in Brighton with a freedom I would never have dreamt possible. I do voluntary work with men and women who are HIV+ or have AIDS and I enjoy seeing my old flames!'

Bob was born in 1929, came to Brighton in 1959 from Worthing. 'I've had many jobs and several different careers. I'm happily settled in Saltdean with my partner and a close circle of friends. Brighton was very lively in the sixties - either the town's losing its vitality or I am.'

Bobby was born in 1938 in Boston, Massachusetts and moved to England when she was eight. Visitor to Brighton during the sixties. Worked as a painter and teacher. Now resident mainly in France and working towards an exhibition in Montpellier in 1993.

Buck was born in the East End of London 1926. 'I am a Capricorn, easy-going, hard-working and enjoy life. I've worked most of my life in catering. Now retired. I hope there's a few more years yet to enjoy.'

David Nott: 'I was born in 1939, a working-class boy from suburban Hertfordshire. An actor as a young man, I first came to Brighton to work in 1962 and stayed on and off throughout the sixties. I'm a writer now and live in South London. The older I've got, the more I've come to terms with being gay and it doesn't bother me now.'

Dennis Houldsworth was born in the Yorkshire Dales and has been a regular visitor to Brighton since 1955. Moved here in 1972. Worked as a chef for most of his life. Likes Brighton for its people and its laid-back attitude.

Eddie was born in Dublin in 1942. Came to Brighton in 1959 to join his father. Done more jobs than he can remember.

Edward was born 1919. Came to Brighton with his partner frequently throughout the sixties. Settled here in 1971 and has since been very active in the local gay movement.

Eric Oliver was born in Bromley in 1914. Came to Brighton in 1958 and worked as a porter at the Royal Sussex County Hospital until his retirement. Now a permanent resident of the Men's Beach at Shoreham.

George was born in Dublin in 1936. Worked as a shop assistant. Resident of Hove during the fifties and sixties. Now happy and liberated.

Gerald was born in Brighton and is still very happily living here. Worked in the field of popular modern music. Recently retired.

Gill was born in 1934 in Newcastle-under-Lyme. Resident of Brighton in the fifties and sixties. Worked in her own poodle-trimming business. Now living a contented life with Sheila and proud of their shared achievements.

Grant was born in Kent in 1916. Rejected by the military for war service, came to Brighton for his health shortly after the war, and worked for twenty-five years in the voluntary services as an accountant. Now retired.

Harriet was born in 1922 in Middleton-in-Teesdale. Resident of Hove in the sixties. Worked at various occupations, mostly involving driving/outdoor work. Now retired, relaxed and mother to five cats.

Harry: 'I'm from Nantwich in Cheshire and settled in Brighton in 1958, resumed a career in nursing and stayed in it until my retirement. I go to painting classes and do a lot of reading which I've never had time to do before.'

Helen Jarvis was born in 1924 in Leicester. During the sixties, was a visitor to Brighton and worked as a journalist on a Brighton newspaper. Still writing. . .

Henry was born in Southend in 1908. Moved to Worthing as a boy. Worked as a chauffeur all his life. Lived in nursing homes in and around Brighton since his retirement.

James is now sixty and has lived in Brighton all his life. After a number of jobs locally, he now teaches in London. His hobbies include collecting cigarette cards, and he loves Brighton because of its liberal, tolerant history.

Jan: 'I was born in St Albans in 1943 and grew up in Clacton, Essex. I did various jobs until nurse training RNMH. I was an occasional visitor to Brighton in the late sixties. I've had three long-term relationships and after my last partner died in 1985, I moved to Yorkshire where I've settled and am now living very happily with Louisa.'

Janice was born in 1944 in Hove. Visitor to Brighton during the sixties. Has run a lesbian club in London and now lives in the West Country.

Janine Sammons was born in 1934 in Sussex Square, Brighton. Hospital Admissions Officer during the fifties, then Psychiatric Social Worker. Visited Brighton during the fifties and sixties. Now a full-time (and very mature) art student and currently Resident Artist at Kew Studios.

Joanne Taylor (claims to have been) born in the early thirties in Stepney, East London - true Cockney. Worked in the travel business and advertising. Visitor to Brighton in the fifties and sixties. Now a music presenter and promoter with her own roadshow.

John D Stamford was born in Lancashire in 1939. Came to Brighton in the sixties and established Spartacus magazine. Now living abroad and working as director and editor-in-chief of Spartacus Gay Guide.

Kay Dick was born in 1915 in London. Visitor to Rottingdean during the fifties and resident of Brighton in the late sixties. Author, editor, reviewer, first woman director in English publishing. About to start work on an autobiographical work which will be entitled, 'The Fiction of My Life'.

Margaret Kent was born in 1927 in Croydon. Worked as a bank cashier. Visitor to Brighton during the fifties and sixties. Now retired.

Michael Lowrie was born in 1938 in Luton. Escaped to Brighton in 1960 and worked in a Wimpey Bar. Worked in several factories as a clothing cutter, then drifted into all sorts of things. Currently unemployed.

Jocelyn Morris was born in London in 1922. She was a visitor to Brighton in the fifties and sixties and worked as a floor manager and production assistant with the BBC TV drama department. Now retired, she enjoys writing and gardening.

Patrick Newley: 'I was born in Dublin in 1955, son of the distinguished Irish poet and playwright Patrick Galvin. I started at The Unicorn Bookshop in Brighton, moved to Better Books to work for John Calder, became an actor, had my own column on the Sunday Times for two years, assistant editor of Q International, editor of Video Viewer, press agent for Dougie Byng, Robin Maugham, Jim Bailey, personal manager for Mrs. Shufflewick, contributor to the gay press of 21 years standing. Currently editor of Scandal and correspondent for Newsgroup Newspapers. Recently completed my autobiography.'

Peter: 'I'm a 67 year old passive quean, now retired, or retarded as you wish. I've been a professional all my life and in spite of a touch of gout, I think I still am. I find people most interesting, that is, those that are still alive. A lot of the characters now have gone. But I still enjoy the scene. I've been lucky. I've survived. Thank God.'

Richard was born in Birmingham in 1940. 'Came to Brighton with my first boyfriend in 1963 and we both got jobs on the buses for the summer. Have lived in the South ever since. Having lived a gay life until 1979, I was married for four and a half years and have since lived alone. Now work in the retail trade and live a quiet and fulfilled life. Still looking for the right one, the real thing.'

Sandie was born in 1939 in Birmingham. Resident of Brighton in the sixties. Worked in teaching and personnel management. 'I'm very happy that gay people are more accepted now but I think that blatant behaviour is unnecessary because being gay is part of life.'

Sheila Twell was born in Brighton in 1930 and has lived here ever since. 'I worked as a hairdresser for twenty-five years and hated every minute of it! I have quietly achieved all the goals I have set myself. Gill and I now enjoy a full and varied social life with friends of all persuasions.'

Siobhan was born in 1948 in Dublin. Visitor to Brighton

in the late sixties. Worked as a forecourt attendant. Now lives in Brighton. 'I want lesbians not to have to suffer the isolation I felt in my early days and feel that Section 28 damages everybody's all-round education.

Steven was born in London in 1950. Came to Brighton as a lark with a mate in 1965 and never went back. Done various jobs. Now working very hard for gay causes.

Ted was born in Southampton in 1948. 'I came to Brighton in 1967, aged nineteen years and very innocent - green even. Took a degree in Chemistry at Brighton Polytechnic. Since then I have worked as a chemist, ran my own pub and am now a bar/catering manager in Brighton. I stayed because I found love in Brighton and Brighton is me.'

Valerie was born in 1934 in Leicester. In the WRAF in the fifties and then did market research for various companies. Visitor to Brighton during the fifties and sixties. Now living near Brighton with her life-long friend and still doing market research when the recession lets her.

Vera was born in 1918 in Newmarket. Worked in the travel business, in advertising and for many years as a customer relations rep. for a large company. Visitor to Brighton during the fifties and sixties. Waiting to win the pools so she can afford some of life's little luxuries!

Vicky was born in 1939 in Romford. Has been a business woman nearly all her life - left school without any qualifications and still managed to make some money! Visitor to Brighton during the late fifties and sixties. Now a Brighton resident, living a happy, quiet home life.

Glossary

affair lover.

baby butch young butch lesbian.

bona good or fab.

butch masculine lesbian.

cartso male genitals, also **cartes**.

chicken young gay man, also **chicken-snatcher**.

come out, come over to reveal one's own or to acknowledge another's homosexuality.

cottage public lavatory used as a meeting place, also to **cottage**.

cruet male genitals.

diesel heavy butch, also **diesel-dyke**.

dyke lesbian.

fag-hag straight woman with a penchant for gay male company, also **quean's moll.**

family the homosexual community.

fem feminine lesbian.

Gateways legendary basement lesbian club in Chelsea, London, now closed. Parts of 'The Killing of Sister George' filmed here.

gay switchboards telephone lines offering advice and information to lesbians and gay men. Brighton Lesbian Line 603298, London Lesbian Line 071 251 6911, London Lesbian and Gay Switchboard 071 837 7324, Brighton Gay Switchboard 690825.

the gear, the regalia butch lesbian clothes.

lallies legs.

nanty none or nothing.

normal heterosexual.

omi man.

palone woman.

polari gay slang or to speak in gay slang.

quean camp gay man (c. 1960 frequent alternative spelling to queen.)

rent prostitution, also **rent-boy**.

riah hair.

Robin Hood lesbian club in Bayswater, London.

slap make-up.

trade male sexual partner or the act of sex with a partner.

troll to seek sexual partners, to cruise, hence **trolling-ground**.

vada to look.

(Many gay words and phrases of the period, such as **camp**, **tatty**, **drag**, **naff**, **send up**, **gay**, have passed into general heterosexual parlance.)

Brighton Ourstory Project

'Daring Hearts' is the latest production by Brighton Ourstory Project. It has been published in conjunction with QueenSpark Books.

Brighton Ourstory Project is a group of lesbians and gay men committed to ensuring that our lesbian and gay lives are recorded, known and valued.

'Daring Hearts' is born out of a living memory archive of material which ranges from taped interviews, transcripts and photographs to pulp fiction, newspapers and magazines. It is one of several projects aimed at making our roots and experiences accessible to all generations of ourselves.

Our previous projects have included:

Really Living - a mixed media performance of Brighton's lesbian and gay past. Brighton Festival 1990.

Articles in various magazines including Square Peg and Gay Times.

Walky Talky - a guided tour of Brighton revealing the incredible truths (and some of the infamous legends) behind the town's Regency facade. Brighton Pride 1990/1991.

A Community Hidden Even From Itself - talk given to the Federation of Worker Writers and Community Publishers. Ruskin College, Oxford. November 1991.

Brighton Ourstory Project is not funded. We are not a charity nor are we aligned to any official institution. If you feel you could contribute to the Project, be it with your money, your time or your stories, we'd be delighted to hear from you. All communications are strictly confidential!

Brighton Ourstory Project are: Beccie Mannall, Jill, Jim Martin, Joyce Chester, Larry Berryman, Linda Pointing, Peter Dennis, Tom Sargant.

Acknowledgements

Many thanks to all our contributors.

Also: Al Thomson, Andy Fisher, Annie, Arthur Law, Carmel Kelly, Carol, Clare Caardus, Dani Ahrens, Hilary, Jo Taylor, John Cockerill, Ken McLaughlin, Lil and Mike Lloyd, Matt Williams, Monica, Peter Burton, Ruth Sykes, Sue May, Tony Stuart, Brighton and Hove Women's Centre, Brighton Council Planning Department, the Black Horse pub.

Special thanks to Nick Osmond for his time and support and to Melita Dennett for rescuing us from the typesetting.

Margin photograph of Kay Dick by Michael Wagen.
Line drawings by Larry Berryman.

Brighton Ourstory Project
PO Box 449
Brighton
BN1 1UU

QueenSpark Books

QueenSpark have published this book because we believe that the printed word has a unique authority. Publishing means power; most people are excluded from this magic circle.

The aim of QueenSpark Books is to make writing and publishing more democratic and to give visibility to the history of everyday life and 'ordinary' people. We run a number of co-operative writing groups and have published books by a few of the millions of people whose social and educational background deny them a public voice.

One group of people who, at least until very recently, have always been silenced by our society and treated as if they were invisible, is the lesbian and gay community. They have been refused the right to be themselves. This book is another step on their way to claiming that right.

The first QueenSpark Book was by Albert Paul, a Brighton carpenter-joiner of seventy who wrote it on seven successive Tuesdays when his wife was out. Since then we have published over thirty books.

Our authors often say they can't imagine how anyone could be interested in their stories, but their success shows that people do have a need and an appetite for books which give shape, purpose and meaning to an experience which they know and share themselves.

We hope our lesbian and gay readers will find themselves in this book, even if they weren't around in the fifties and sixties. We hope our straight readers, whilst discovering that the contributors, in all their diversity, are racy and resilient, compassionate, brave, life-loving and occasionally outrageous, will also recognise that they aren't all that different from themselves.

We also publish works of oral history and *Daring Hearts* is an outstanding example of this kind of book. The contributors have found a written voice through lovingly edited transcriptions from a sound archive which is itself an irreplaceable record of how it felt to be lesbian or gay in Brighton in the fifties and sixties.

Our current publications include *Everything seems smaller* by Sid Manville, *Moulsecoomb Days* by Ruby Dunn, *Pullman Attendant* by Bert Hollick, *At the Pawnbrokers* by Lillie Morgan, *Little Ethel Smith* by herself and *Pullman Craftsmen*, an important oral history book about life in the Brighton Pullman Workshop after the war.

We have a part-time paid worker but are run mainly by volunteers. If you would like to join a writing group, send some of your work for us to read, or just help out, please do get in touch. Our office is staffed on Mondays.

QueenSpark Books
68 Grand Parade
Brighton
BN2 2 JY
Tel. 571916